Presented To

. . . .

From

. . . .

Date

. . . .

America's Teacher™ VICKI CARUANA is foremost a teacher, speaking at educational and homeschool conferences nationwide. She is a frequent guest on various radio and television broadcasts and her writing appears in many magazines. Vicki is the founder of *Teachers in Prayer,* and she lives in Colorado Springs, Colorado.

APPLES

OF

GOLD

FOR TEACHERS

VICKI CARUANA

BETHANY HOUSE PUBLISHERS

Minneapolis, Minnesota

Published by Bethany House Publishers
11400 Hampshire Avenue South
Bloomington, Minnesota 55438
www.bethanyhouse.com

Bethany House Publishers is a Division of
Baker Book House Company, Grand Rapids, Michigan.

Printed in the United States of America

Library of Congress Cataloging-in-Publication Data

Caruana, Vicki.
    Apples of gold for teachers / by Vicki Caruana.
        p.   cm.
    ISBN 0–7642–2792–0 (hardcover : alk. paper)
    1. Teachers—Conduct of life.   2. Teaching—Religious aspects—Christianity.
I. Title.
    LB1775.C348   2003
        371.1—dc21   2003013795

To my mother,

Eileen,

my first and best teacher,

from whom I continue to learn.

Mc DIVITT SCHOOL
OLD BRIDGE   N J

GRADE 3

MRS   KURTZ

SPI   1972

ACKNOWLEDGMENTS

I would like to thank Steve Laube—my editor, my friend, and now my agent—someone whose vision is so clear. Without it, this book would not have been possible.

I would like to thank Carol Kurtz, my third grade teacher from McDivitt Elementary in Old Bridge, New Jersey, whose love for teaching permeated my soul in such a way that my love for learning is a direct result. Thank you, Mrs. Kurtz!

Note: That's Vicki in the center of the front row.

CONTENTS

INTRODUCTION

Are you thirsting to live a deeper life? Are you painfully aware that as a teacher your life is hard for anyone outside of teaching to understand? Even though all that we go through is common to humankind, it's always nice when someone comes along who knows what our life is like firsthand and ministers to us. That's what I want to do for you here in the pages of *Apples of Gold for Teachers*.

Teachers have a lot to complain about and are justified in their complaints. But we have to be careful we do not become known as a group of complainers. When the Israelites continually complained after they left Egypt, God caused them to wander and wait to enter the Promised Land until that generation died. You may be wandering in the desert right now. God is waiting for you to come to Him for rest and to pursue the path of wisdom.

Allow God's Word to refresh you and to sustain you. Every child you teach will benefit from your own purposeful following of the Word of God. Take it from someone who knows what your life is like: You can't afford not to. There are too many people counting on you—and hopefully when they look at you, they will experience the love of Christ.

Each of these fifty meditations draws you into God's Word, offers you a personal parable from the classroom, and then shows you how to apply these apples of gold to your life. The "Daily Apples" I offer are practical ways you can become a teacher God can use.

Share the Blessing!
Vicki Caruana

I

BE OF GOOD COURAGE

An Apple of Gold

*Have I not commanded you? Be strong and courageous. Do not be
terrified; do not be discouraged, for the Lord your God will be with
you wherever you go.*

JOSHUA 1:9

Sowing the Seed

Joshua, successor of Moses, had a monumental job ahead of
him. The Israelites were still mourning Moses' death when God
appointed Joshua to lead the nation. He had to lead two million
people into a strange new land and conquer it. Joshua was prepared, since he had assisted Moses for many years, but he still
must have had moments of trepidation and questions.

*Will they all follow me? Am I really equipped to lead them? I know God
is capable of conquering those already in the land, but am I? What if I fail?*

God knew Joshua's heart. He knew his concerns and heard his
unspoken questions. God assured Joshua that He would be with
him just as He was with Moses. God would do what He promised: He would bring them into the land that He swore to their
fathers before them. Joshua had to trust God to do what He said
He would do and to follow the Law. But was it enough?

God commands us to be strong and to have courage. Even
when the obstacles are many and our enemies are formidable. God
is with us wherever we go.

Tending the Orchard

We frequently experience changes in leadership in the field of education. New principals often worry that not all the teachers will follow their lead. In fact, many teachers leave a school along with an exiting principal. And it is discouraging. Teachers often experience feelings of inadequacy. I excelled in my teacher preparation program and learned alongside some of the best supervising teachers during my internship, but I remember how painfully inadequate and unprepared I felt when I was assigned my first class. It was what I wanted. It was what I was trained to do. To me, having my own classroom was the "promised land." Yet I trembled in anticipation of it.

In those times, when the land seems alien and we are called to lead, we can remember that God is with us. Each day we face new challenges, troubled students, and difficult parents. *Be not afraid.* "I will never leave you nor forsake you" (Joshua 1:5).

I admit that there is much to fear in our country today. It is not at all like in the days of our own fathers. Yet God is the same. The promise is the same. And with Him we can conquer many of life's challenges.

Reaping the Harvest

Today you may be standing on the hillside overlooking the "promised land," wondering if it is safe to enter. Changing schools, teaching a new subject, or becoming a teacher for the very first time can sometimes make you feel ill-equipped, insignificant, and even unable. The truth is, you are prepared, you are of pivotal importance, and you are able—with God you are all that and more. Focus on the truth and follow God's command. *Be not afraid nor dismayed!*

Daily Apple

Seven Affirmations of Teachers

These seven affirmations are provided by the Daily Apples Web site: *www.dailyapples.com*. I have added one of my own to the beginning of this list that I encourage you to remember before anything else:

God is with me!

1. I am proud to be a teacher.
2. Teaching is one of the most honorable and noble of all professions.
3. I love what I do and know that my enthusiasm is contagious.
4. I bring knowledge, dedication, and understanding to my classroom.
5. I make a positive difference in my students' lives.
6. My students will be better people because of me, and I will be a better person because of them.
7. I know what I give to my students will come back to me in many wonderful and unexpected ways.

2

TALK SO KIDS WILL LISTEN

An Apple of Gold

*Take note of this: Everyone should be quick to listen,
slow to speak and slow to become angry, for man's anger
does not bring about the righteous life that God desires.*

JAMES 1:19–20

Sowing the Seed

Some of us like the sound of our own voices. We are great talkers, but sometimes we forget to listen. Too much talking and too little listening tells others that we think our ideas are more important than theirs. James advises us to monitor our talking and become aware of how much we talk and how much we listen. When people talk with you, do they feel that their viewpoints are valued?

Some of us prefer our own opinions over those of others. If someone doesn't agree with us, we erupt in anger because our egos are bruised. We raise our voices as if to say, "I am hurt" or "My opinions are not being heard." There is such a thing as righteous anger, but this isn't it. Be wary of selfish anger.

Tending the Orchard

My first two years of teaching were filled with yelling. I couldn't seem to get away from yelling at my students to maintain order in the classroom. There were raised voices in my house growing up. Sometimes that's what it took to quiet the five of us down. But when I tried this same strategy on thirty sixth graders, it made little to no impact.

I wasn't alone. I could hear the eighth-grade English teacher next door yelling at the top of his lungs, too. The flip side of this whole fiasco was that I had a strong desire to have my students like me. I couldn't see that happening in the current climate of my classroom.

Some of the advice I received as a beginner teacher didn't seem to foster positive relationships with students: "Don't smile before Christmas" and "Don't let them get away with anything" were mentioned again and again to me by veteran teachers. I was miserable, and so were my students.

Gaining control through intimidation isn't healthy—even for the intimidator! The volume of my yelling that made students behave one day didn't work the next. I had to keep raising the decibel level day after day. Sometimes when my students had gone for the day, I would break down and cry and wonder why I ever thought I could be a teacher.

No one taught me how to deal with this in college.

Then, during a workshop about "modeling the love of learning to students," I discovered a technique to quiet rambunctious youngsters without raising my voice. It worked! My days of yelling were over.

When I finally had peace and quiet and could really think about my situation, I realized that *listening* to my students had never occurred to me. Why were they so rowdy? Why did their voices lift to unprecedented heights? Why didn't they listen to *me*? The answer lay in the fact that I believed teaching them was all about me: They were the lucky recipients of my wisdom! I believed they should be open and willing to receive all that I had to give them.

I had to change what I believed to be true before I could change my actions and, ultimately, their responses.

Reaping the Harvest

Talk so that kids will listen. Listen so that kids will talk. Do each with love, patience, and kindness. Value them enough to put their needs before your own.

Daily Apple

A Free Public Education

"Be sure that no children in your classroom are ever embarrassed because their families are on a strict budget."

This phrase, which is included in every state's statute on education, is largely ignored. Our school supply lists for students keep getting longer. Then we ask them to bring in more items sometime in February. Respect parents' pocketbooks. Limit requests for money or supplies. It's unfair to assume that all families can afford a particular calculator or an expensive field trip.

3

DARKNESS AND LIGHT

An Apple of Gold

Therefore judge nothing before the appointed time; wait till the Lord comes. He will bring to light what is hidden in darkness and will expose the motives of men's hearts. At that time each will receive his praise from God.

1 CORINTHIANS 4:5

Sowing the Seed

If we're not careful, arrogance can grip our hearts. The church at Corinth was admonished by Paul not to judge whether or not another Christian was a good follower of Christ. Later, in chapter 5, Paul gives instruction about when and how to confront those in the church who are sinning. We are all in a different place in the continuum of sanctification. On our way to maturity, we find ourselves looking at those around us to see where they are on their journey—comparing ourselves to them. But things often are hidden from us, and it isn't our job to bring them out into the light. God will do so in His own predetermined time. He will reveal the purposes of each heart—even our own.

What is our job, then? It is to keep our eyes focused on our own progression toward maturity in Christ. "Set your minds on things above, not on earthly things" (Colossians 3:2). When we're tempted to look away from our own path and onto that of a friend or colleague, our mind becomes set on the things of the earth.

Tending the Orchard

Cathy taught at our school longer than any other teacher. We all saw her as the matriarch of our faculty. After thirty years in one school, she had seen a thing or two. We all heard the stories, and after a while I decided I didn't want to become one of her "stories" to tell to future teachers.

It seemed that Cathy's stories focused on what other teachers and administrators did wrong, in her eyes. There was the time a new transfer to our school didn't plan a grade-wide field trip according to procedure. And then a particularly strict fifth-grade teacher didn't receive any Christmas presents from her students. "Served her right," Cathy announced to us during recess duty.

I heard pronouncements like "If the principal only knew what she was up to" or "You can certainly tell he's right out of college." Cathy's comments weren't intended to help us avoid mistakes, but to elevate her standing in the eyes of others. Yet my opinion of Cathy's maturity as an educator was progressing toward one of indifference, even disgust.

I had two choices, as I saw it. I could keep quiet and avoid her, or I could speak up and try to nurture a friendship with her. Avoidance felt like the safest route, until I realized that would only guarantee I would be her next "object lesson." I spoke up.

Cathy professed to be a Christian. I did not rebuke her, but instead followed her comments with some of my own. I would say, "Since the principal doesn't know, maybe we could counsel her to do what is right instead" or "I remember being right out of college. Teaching wasn't at all what I expected. Sounds like he needs a mentor." Eventually Cathy was able to see that she could use her status as a veteran teacher to bring others along and not put them down.

Reaping the Harvest

We are often touted as the *expert* by those outside of our own school. That expert status can make it difficult to see our own flaws, and instead we look critically at other teachers. If another teacher is either choosing the wrong path or is not up to the task of teaching, look for ways to build her up and support her. At the right time, God will reveal what is hidden in the darkness. In the meantime, make sure what you do is always in the light.

Daily Apple

Offering *specific praise* is not only important with regard to students. It is a powerful tool to use with adults, as well. Look for ways to encourage other teachers who might be struggling. What are they doing *right*? What do you like about how they teach? Some teachers dislike public attention (as do some students), so they benefit more from one-on-one attention. Maybe while standing in line together to buy lunch, you could say something like "Great choice for a field trip. It ties right in to this quarter's lesson."

4

BUSYBODIES

An Apple of Gold

And that ye study to be quiet, and to do your own business, and to work with your own hands, as we commanded you; that ye may walk honestly toward them that are without, and that ye may have lack of nothing.

1 THESSALONIANS 4:11–12 KJV

Sowing the Seed

The church is full of busybodies! It was then just as it is now. Maybe the Christians in Thessalonica had too much time on their hands, so that they found themselves paying more attention to the business of others than to their own. Paul reminds them (and us) of three things they must do instead and then offers a promise to go with it. *Study to be quiet* is more than just being quiet. When you study something, you learn as much about it as you can and then consciously apply it to your life. We've been instructed how to speak in many instances in the Bible, but here we are instructed how to be quiet. *To do your own business* is a command to take care of our own responsibilities, not those of others. *To work with your own hands* is focused effort on the work we are each called to do.

The promise is that when we walk honestly before those who are without Christ, they will look at us and see Christ, and we will lack nothing when it comes time to speak and to minister to them. But this can only happen if we are focused on what God has called us to do and we don't get *off task*.

Tending the Orchard

I know that my growth as both a teacher and a Christian depends upon how much effort I put into seeking opportunities for growth. Schools can easily become dens of complaint instead of nests of learning. I remember what it was like in the teachers' lounge or the staff lunchroom. I remember the gossip and the grumbling. It can spill out into the hallways, at the mailboxes, and onto the playgrounds if we're not careful. And careful we must be.

Studying to be quiet is somewhat of a challenge to most teachers. Teachers are talkers by nature. It's what allows us to communicate knowledge to our students. But it can also get us into trouble. Our districts and schools discourage talking outside of school. We're not to talk to the press about what is wrong in our schools. We're not to talk to parents about problems. We're supposed to be quiet. In a way, this is good advice.

This is not to say that the public doesn't have a right to know what goes on in their "public" schools, but if all we do is talk, gossip, and complain, nothing productive gets done. Our jobs, as I see it, are to follow the path Paul outlined to the Thessalonians. *Do our own business*—the business of teaching and coaching children toward success. *Work with our own hands*—do what we're supposed to do—create and plan lessons, teach, grade work, counsel children, take an active part in a school committee, communicate with parents, etc.

Reaping the Harvest

The work we do as teachers is important work. We are joined

with God in His work. He expects us to mind our own business and do what He's called us to do in a way that honors Him. Teach heartily as unto the Lord!

Daily Apple

Become an inveterate note writer. Keep a stack of note paper on your desk. Make a commitment to recognize good deeds performed by students, colleagues, custodians, secretaries, administrators, librarians, aides, parents, or volunteers. Five minutes spent each day sending a couple of thoughtful notes will pay big dividends and contribute to making your school a more pleasant place to teach.[1]

5

WHERE ARE YOU ROOTED?

An Apple of Gold
He will be like a tree planted by the water
that sends out its roots by the stream.
It does not fear when heat comes;
its leaves are always green.
It has no worries in a year of drought
and never fails to bear fruit.

JEREMIAH 17:8

Sowing the Seed

Where we live in Colorado, it gets pretty dry. In fact, this year we had the worst drought since the 1800s. Yet I'm always amazed and intrigued when I fly over the plains and see strips of green and trees etched on the landscape like the close-to-the-surface veins in my great-aunt's delicate hands. There's water down there somewhere. And in the not-so-recent history, there were probably creeks and rivers running through the now empty and at times desolate plains of eastern Colorado. *How do the trees tolerate it?* I wonder. *How do they retain their brilliant green when I can't see their water source?* Did the trees spring up as a result of the water or were they planted at the water's edge more than one hundred years ago? They have tapped into a water source so deep that even the worst drought in our state's history couldn't dry it up.

That is how it must be for us if we are to survive, and even thrive. In our case, the tree was planted; it didn't spring up on its own. Who planted it? God, the Creator. When we are reborn into His family, He plants us at the edge of Living Water, where our roots can tap into the underground river that never ends. It is our life source. It is what sustains us. It is not affected by drought. It can withstand whatever people do to nature and whatever nature does to people. The problem comes when we look around us and see there is a drought and forget where our roots lie.

We can be sure that we were planted by the water and that even when we are surrounded by desolation, we can remain green and bear fruit. Others will look with wonder at the tree in full bloom in the middle of what looks like dried-up, barren ground. They will ask, "Where is its water source?" The source is what it's all about.

Tending the Orchard

The isolation of teaching can very often feel like a desolate wasteland. Students aren't achieving as much as we'd hoped. Parents are absent, except when they want to file a complaint. Colleagues come together once a day during lunch and vent on one another. Principals and other administrators make demands that sometimes seem impossible. And the public—well, in their eyes, we are the source of all their problems.

I was close to burnout when I finally learned the secret to longevity in this profession: Reliance on my faith was all that could sustain me. I found this out only after looking for sources of strength and sustenance from other places and people. I love to walk, so I made it a priority to walk every day to stay in tip-top condition. I love to read, so I set aside time every day to read just for pleasure. I love crafts, so I made sure I was always making something to give to someone else. I love gardening, so I planted and nurtured a garden in the small plot our condo association allowed me. Yet none of these things helped ward off the discouragement and weariness I began to feel day after day at school.

From before the beginning of my teaching career I was known to others as a woman of faith. But looking back now, I see that I only brought that faith out on special occasions. It was a separate piece of my identity. I kept it in a treasure box and used it as a last resort. A tree that is watered only when it looks like it is dying will not thrive. It may survive, but just barely. We can tap into the Living Water purposely. A tree's roots grow after its water source, so too can our faith. Make time everyday to feed on the Word of God. Praise God daily for your life source. Look for ways to spread the Gospel right where you're planted!

Reaping the Harvest

Changing our focus on what and who sustains us can change lives—ours and those we are called to teach. Who knows? Someday a child or his parent may ask, "How can you be so peaceful in the middle of this situation?" That's when you can share the water with them.

Daily Apple

Sometimes we struggle to remember why we went into teaching to begin with. Usually we had a teacher who made a positive impact on our lives. They were our mentors. In his book *The Courage to Teach,*[1] Parker J. Palmer says, "If we discovered a teacher's heart in ourselves by meeting a great teacher, recalling that meeting may help us take heart in teaching once more."

We need to be reminded what makes a quality teacher so we can become one. Think back to your own school days. Who made a difference in your life? And the next time you're in the teachers' lounge or lunchroom, ask the question aloud to your table mates. It can brighten a discouraging day!

6

WORD SMART

An Apple of Gold

*When you are brought before synagogues, rulers and authorities,
do not worry about how you will defend yourselves or what
you will say, for the Holy Spirit will teach you
at that time what you should say.*

LUKE 12:11–12

Sowing the Seed

The disciples had the best preparation of anyone to speak for God. They had Jesus himself to teach them! They also knew first-hand how to practically apply God's Word during their time of apostolic work. But even they knew they couldn't go toe to toe with well-educated Jewish leaders and dominate the conversation. In this passage, Jesus prepares them for this eventuality. After Jesus' resurrection, the disciples would be challenged for the words they spoke. They would be brought before judges and kings and rabbis all looking for ways to discredit them, and worse. How could they possibly prepare for that?

Jesus tells us not to worry about what will happen in this arena. We will be confronted. Our faith will be challenged. Our words will be disputed. What will we say? How will we answer? The Holy Spirit will give us the words we need when we need them. That was His promise. But it is important to remember that this is not a passive responsibility. As the disciples were prepared, so must we be. We must study God's Word, and then God will bring His truths to mind just when we need them. Pray before you even open your mouth, *"Lord, choose my words and guide my tongue and give them ears to hear."*

Tending the Orchard

Even as an adult, getting called into the principal's office can be unnerving—and it happened to me more than once that year! I returned to the classroom after a five-year absence and found myself confronted at almost every turn either about my beliefs or what I thought was "right." The first time the principal called me in, I had no reason to suspect I would be ambushed.

"Mrs. Caruana, why did you tell parents you were in need of additional supplies?" she asked while looking at me like I was enemy number one!

"Because I am out of supplies, and we can't order more. I'm out of copy paper, file folders, and dry erase markers. We also need shoeboxes for our science projects, newspapers for current events, and poster board for displays." I decided my explanation was appropriate.

I was wrong.

"We don't tell parents that we're low on supplies. We don't ask them for additional materials!" she bellowed.

"You would rather students go without?" I asked naïvely.

"It is your job to make what we give you last through the year. Now you've opened up this school to scrutiny that I would have preferred we didn't receive."

I sat there waiting for her to say something like "Go to your room, young lady!" but instead she asked her secretary to escort me out.

"From now on, Mrs. Caruana, any and all communication

you have with parents must be cleared through me first," she said while writing furiously and not looking up at me.

I was humiliated. I was crushed. I was speechless.

This was the first of many times I ended up in the principal's office. But I was more prepared on the subsequent times. I realized that my response had not been the result of a humble and submissive spirit. Coming up with a quick comeback may be applauded by other teachers, but it wasn't what God wanted. After all, it is His reputation on the line; His that matters, not mine. I needed to study His Word so that I would know how to answer everyone, whether principal, school board member, parent, newspaper reporter, or member of a congressional committee.

Reaping the Harvest

There will be countless opportunities as a teacher to speak for God. Prepare yourself with His Word and then trust that He will give you just the right words when you need them.

Daily Apple

Humor in the classroom is not something that is taught in teacher preparation programs. Yet it is powerful when used wisely. Kids laugh at almost anything. They definitely laugh at our mistakes as teachers, whether we mispronounce something or drop something or have some senior moment right in front of them. We can use these moments to our advantage if we choose. We can use them to build relationship with our students.

The following "Do's and Don'ts for Humor" were taken from *Laughing Lessons* by Ron Burgess[1]:

> *Don't* say you don't have a sense of humor. Everyone does. Everyone's sense of humor is unique. Just like fingerprints

and snowflakes, no two are alike.

Don't be afraid to use humor. Humor, like most things in life, is not an exact science. You have to work at it and play with it to be successful.

Don't be afraid of bombing. Highly paid professionals bomb every day.

Don't let a day go by without a chance to share laughter with your students. Seeing kids smile and hearing them laugh shows your classroom is an inviting, fun place to be.

Do relax, grin, smile, and laugh along with your students. You've got their attention—now teach them!

STORYTIME

An Apple of Gold

I will open my mouth in parables,
I will utter hidden things, things from of old—
what we have heard and known,
what our fathers have told us.
We will not hide them from their children;
we will tell the next generation
the praiseworthy deeds of the Lord,
his power, and the wonders he has done.

PSALM 78:2–4

Sowing the Seed

Stories are the principle technique used in the Bible to impart the truth. Even before the Bible became what it is to us today, prophets, kings, and Jewish leaders taught the Israelites about God and His promises using stories. In this particular passage from the Psalms, Asaph retells the history of the Jewish nation from the time of its slavery in Egypt to David's reign. This passage gives the listener or reader the motivation behind the telling of the story that is to come. Usually the reason is so that we can avoid the same errors as those in the story.

Jesus taught using parables. He must have been a great storyteller, full of energy and animation when He spoke. He held the attention of His audience and often spurred them on into action.

Not everyone who heard His stories chose to walk the path He outlined for them, but at least they couldn't claim later on that they didn't know. Another reason stories are used to communicate truth is that they may be less threatening to an already hostile listener, and Jesus had plenty of those.

Tending the Orchard

During my teacher preparation coursework in college, I took a class that became for me one of the most enjoyable experiences of my life. It was called "Literature for the Child." We surveyed both traditional and contemporary children's literature. We created lessons around literature themes. And we performed many of the stories in front of an audience. We learned and practiced the art of storytelling. This was very intimidating to me.

The first story I told in public was the fable *Three Billy Goats Gruff*. I remember stomping around like the goats going over the bridge under which the terrible troll lived. For the first time I saw eyes that followed me back and forth across the room. I saw faces light up with excitement and understanding. They were engaged. They "got it" when it came to the moral of the story. And they were teachers! Later, when I had my own class, I incorporated the power of story as often as possible. To this day I love the fact that I can light up a room with a story. The best part is that within those stories are nuggets of God's truth. Whether my students are Christian or not, they will "get it."

Reaping the Harvest

Utilize tried and true techniques to infuse excitement into your teaching. Storytelling isn't just for wee ones. Practice your own story. The one that tells who you were before you met Jesus and who you are now that you know Him personally. It is the greatest story ever told!

Daily Apple

Do you have a personal vision for yourself as a teacher? Have you ever thought about it? Your personal beliefs lead you to do what you do each day in and out of the classroom. Try to articulate your personal beliefs, and then decide where you want those beliefs to lead you as a teacher. Just as each student is special and has unique needs, so do teachers. If your principal has never discussed the power of a personal vision with you, take it upon yourself to form one. Once you've created your vision, share it with your principal. Then find ways to open a similar dialogue with your colleagues. "Whether you are a principal, department chair, superintendent, or grade-level leader, regular conversations with everyone you lead can have a significant, positive impact on your organization."[1]

8

HONOR CODE

An Apple of Gold

Be devoted to one another in brotherly love. Honor one another above yourselves. Never be lacking in zeal, but keep your spiritual fervor, serving the Lord. Be joyful in hope, patient in affliction, faithful in prayer. Share with God's people who are in need. Practice hospitality.

ROMANS 12:10–13

Sowing the Seed

In this portion of his letter to the church in Rome, Paul does more than encourage Christians in the way they should behave toward one another. He issues commands about how we should live. *Hate what is evil. Cling to what is good* (v. 9). But then he goes on to outline the attitudes we must have as we do all the things we are called to do. He tells us the ways in which we can honor one another. We don't do it for our own gain but out of God's love.

Our motives dictate whether or not *how* we do what we do pleases God. We are so competitive by nature that it can be difficult to do things for others for purely selfless reasons. Yet we must try. Paul isn't offering suggestions; he's issuing commands! We have reason to honor people: because all people are created in God's image; because other Christians are our brothers and sisters in Christ; and because our Christian brothers and sisters have their own contribution to make to the church on Earth.

Honor one another. Prefer one another (as the King James

Version says). Rejoice with and for one another. Be patient with one another. Pray continuously for one another. Meet one another's needs. Extend hospitality to one another. It's a definite "to do" list, but it is more of a reminder of how we should treat one another on a daily basis.

Tending the Orchard

When our oldest child was in second grade, much to my delight, his teacher was a Christian. I was so grateful to God for a sister in Christ during this time. Our children attended public school, and it is often "hit and miss" when it comes to teachers. Having been a Christian teacher in the public schools myself, I knew the great potential this teacher had to influence the lives of her students. It felt like an incredible blessing—at first.

As a sister in Christ, I felt I did extend preference to this teacher and honored her whenever I could. I try to do that for all teachers, but I knew I would be willing to extend grace to this teacher if needed. For some reason she did not feel the same toward me. Maybe I was too enthusiastic about discovering my son's teacher was a fellow believer. Maybe that enthusiasm translated into meddling, in her eyes. I try to be sensitive about the "territorial" needs of teachers, but maybe I overstepped my bounds. I say "maybe," because it was never clear to me why she was harder on my son than most of the other children. Why she didn't return phone calls and didn't acknowledge notes from home.

It is painful when you do all the things Paul commands in this passage of Romans and still hit a brick wall. Maybe that's why they are commands and not suggestions. It is easier to walk away, even from a sister in Christ. I realized toward the end of the school year that my motives were wrong in dealing with this teacher. My goal was to please her and not God. I wanted to win her favor. I wanted her to honor me as a fellow believer in this public school. I wanted all the wrong things.

Looking back, I'm glad I failed. I'm glad my selfish motives weren't rewarded. It's time to move forward with the motive to share the love of God with others, especially with those who share in the inheritance of Christ.

Reaping the Harvest

Strive to honor those around you, giving preference to fellow believers. Strive also to be honorable in all that you say and do. It pleases God and it pleases those with whom we interact.

Daily Apple

Being prepared as a teacher is one important key to success in the classroom. The following ideas are things you can do to get yourself organized:

1. Do a curriculum plan for the year.
2. Have a calendar of events and deadlines.
3. Set up a daily planner so that you know what you need to accomplish each day. (Include what you want to do before school, during your preparation time, and after school.)
4. Use your preparation time to grade papers and prepare materials for lessons. Don't grade every paper. Use your volunteers, grade papers with the students, and set aside a period of time to grade papers yourself—and then stop![1]

9

WORDS TO LIVE BY

An Apple of Gold
A man finds joy in giving an apt reply,
and how good is a timely word!

PROVERBS 15:23

Sowing the Seed

Saying just the right thing at the right moment is not only satisfying to the listener but also to the speaker. Proverbs includes many verses that guide us in how we should speak, what we should say, and when we should say it. Proverbs 12:14 says, "From the fruit of his lips a man is filled with good things as surely as the work of his hands rewards him." As a result of your words, there will be good fruit. If your words are good, so will be the results of those words. Logically, the opposite would also be true. Each of these verses indicates deliberateness on the part of the speaker. Our words should be carefully chosen and prayerfully considered.

Proverbs 24:26 says, "He who gives a right answer kisses the lips" (KJV). A kiss on the lips was a sign of true friendship in Old Testament times. People often think that in order to avoid hurting a friend, they should bend the truth. But the one who gives an honest answer is a true friend. The "right" answer is not always the answer that people want to hear. The right answer is always a truthful answer.

Proverbs 25:11 says, "A word aptly spoken is like apples of gold in settings of silver." The right word at just the right time is precious. It is treasured and highly valued. If the word is "aptly spoken," it is spoken in a manner that fits the situation and the listener.

Tending the Orchard

Words. They are tools of the trade for a teacher. We use them to impart knowledge. We use them to encourage. We use them to discipline. We use them to question current thinking. We use them to build relationships with students, staff, and parents. One wrong word can have a devastating effect. Similarly, *no* words spoken can have a negative impact. But sometimes, just the right word at just the right time can change a life.

I found it a challenge to offer just the right words at the right time to my students when it came to praising them for their efforts. I think I was more afraid of saying the wrong words, so it was easier not to say anything at all.

That changed with Joe. As an eighth grader who had already been left back twice, Joe had no reason to try anymore. But he was in my care for three class periods a day, and I couldn't stand that all he did was put his head down on his desk and sleep through the day. We go into teaching because we love kids and want to make a positive impact on their lives. I didn't know how to reach Joe.

Little by little I noticed that when I would say something to the top of his blond head as a way to stay connected, he would sit up once in a while. It was like he was hungry for the right words. I started to feed him a steady diet of very specific praise, but I did it privately. By the end of the year Joe no longer slept in my class. He didn't get the best grades, but he did begin to care.

Our words show that we care. Sometimes they are exactly what a student needs to "make it."

Reaping the Harvest

As teachers, our words can be life-giving or life-taking. They can wound or they can heal. They can illuminate or darken the souls of our students. They are powerful and should be chosen and spoken with care.

Daily Apple

Getting students excited and focused about learning at the beginning of a class or the beginning of a new lesson is challenging. Consider asking "opening questions" to build a sense of belonging and purpose.

1. Consider the purpose or main goals of your class: To learn? To gain skills necessary to get into college? To think like a mathematician? To develop social skills? To become better writers? To explore new possibilities?
2. Develop three or four questions the answers to which reflect these goals. Then choose a succinct, easy-to-remember answer for each one. For example:

Question	Answer
Why are we here?	To learn
What will we give today?	Our very best
What will we get from today?	Everything we can
What matters?	Math matters
How smart are we?	Very smart
Where are we headed?	The colleges of our choice

3. After students arrive and get settled in, either you or a student stands at the front of the room and recites each question in turn, while the class responds with the answers in unison. Encourage them to respond with enthusiasm![1]

10

TRUST AND OBEY

An Apple of Gold

Trust in the Lord with all thine heart; and lean not unto thine own understanding. In all thy ways acknowledge him, and he shall direct thy paths.

PROVERBS 3:5–6 KJV

Sowing the Seed

Even though we should constantly seek wisdom, our minds do not possess all the answers we need in this life. Which way should we turn? Which choice is best for us? Which path is God's will for us? Sometimes the decisions seem so big and so consequential that we don't trust anyone with it—even God. But God is the only one who does know what is best for us. We can trust Him completely in every choice we make.

How do we learn to trust God? We learn that God, by His very character, is trustworthy. Throughout the Bible we see how God guides His people, yet they do not always follow. God is faithful even when we are not. Personally, I know God is trustworthy by looking at what He has already done in my life. He is consistent. He is worthy of my trust.

Which way should you turn when you are faced with a difficult or life-changing decision? First we can turn to God in prayer. Then we can seek wise counsel through both the Bible and men and women of wisdom in our lives. Then we can follow God's leading, and as He promised, He will make our paths straight. He will guide us and protect us while we are on the path He has set before us. We can count on it!

Tending the Orchard

I felt "called" to teaching. From a very early age, I knew that was what I should do. As a teacher, I always felt I was right where I belonged. But that all changed after the birth of our first son.

I decided to stay home after Christopher was born. It was something my husband and I decided together. Admittedly, I was confronted regularly by peers who questioned my choice to leave teaching and stay at home. "Won't you be bored?" they asked almost daily leading up to my maternity leave date. If you've ever been home with children, especially babies, you know there is absolutely no time to be bored.

After five years at home, I longed for the classroom again. Teaching is a calling and a part of my being. We decided that when Christopher started kindergarten, it would be the right time for me to go back. And I did.

However, within a few weeks I realized it was a mistake. The stress level in our home was ridiculously high. Our younger son, only four years old, was in day care and not handling the separation well. I taught at the school where Christopher attended kindergarten, and even that didn't offer me any comfort. Yet I am a person who always wants to do what is *right*, and what was right was to complete my year-long contract. So I stayed.

For months I agonized over how I had made such a poor choice. My husband and I had carefully considered the impact on our family, especially the financial impact. My previous supervisors offered me a job the moment I inquired if any were available. It seemed that every door had opened on the spot for this move. I boldly walked through them.

As I cried to God about this problem and how stressful it was on all of us, especially our younger child, He gently said, "Now you ask me?" I felt like my New York Italian grandmother was lovingly spooning out her daily dose of guilt.

I hadn't taken my decision before the throne. I hadn't sought the counsel of fellow believers. I hadn't gone to the Bible to seek wisdom. I had made my choice based solely on my expertise and the counsel of other teachers. The desire to teach wasn't wrong, but God had asked me to lay down that desire for a season.

Reaping the Harvest

Bring your decisions directly to God. Scour His Word for guidance. Pursue the counsel of wise men and women. And wait on Him to reveal the path you are to walk. Pray for clarity, but with the understanding that sometimes God expects us to walk in faith even if the way isn't clearly marked out for us.

Daily Apple

View hall duty as an opportunity. It gives you a chance to build positive relationships with students outside the classroom. The efforts will enhance your rapport in the classroom.[1]

11

WHAT'S YOUR PLEASURE?

An Apple of Gold

Nothing is better for a man than that he should eat and drink, and
that his soul should enjoy good in his labor. This also, I saw, was
from the hand of God. For who can eat, or who can have enjoyment,
more than I? For God gives wisdom and knowledge and joy to a
man who is good in His sight; but to the sinner He gives the work
of gathering and collecting, that he may give to him who is good before
God. This also is vanity and grasping for the wind.

ECCLESIASTES 2:24–26 NKJV

Sowing the Seed

Life is complicated. It was no less complicated in King Solomon's day. Sometimes our response to life's complications is to walk away from our responsibilities and have a big irresponsible party. In the passage above, Solomon is not encouraging that kind of pleasure seeking. He is encouraging us to take pleasure in all that we do and in the work of our hands.

Our lives come from God's hand. True enjoyment comes when we follow God's principles for living. Without Him, satisfaction is a fruitless search. Without Him our work is pointless toil and there is no direction for us to navigate through life's complications.

Each day is a gift from God. Solomon tells us to take life one day at a time and thank God for it. Each day is a new chance to serve Him in it. Each day we can find enjoyment, and others will look at us and wonder how, within a tiresome occupation, we can still find joy.

Tending the Orchard

"How do you do it?" my parent volunteer asked after one particularly troublesome day with students.

"I take it one day at a time," I offered. "Sometimes I have to take it one minute at a time." We both laughed, knowing how true that comment really was.

When I taught learning-disabled students in middle school, I often sought high and low for joy in my job. Once I even looked for it as a chair hurtled through the air toward me, thrown by an especially frustrated eighth grader. It wasn't easy to find. At that time I looked at my personal relationship with God as something I had outside of school. School was my domain—my area of expertise.

The days blurred together into one disappointing school year. When the following August came, I still didn't know where I would find the joy I believed would sustain me. But I wasn't ready to cry "Burnout!" just yet. I began to read book after book about avoiding burnout. I chose and attended in-service workshops that promised to help me have a great school year. I remember walking into my classroom that first day back feeling empowered, rested, and rejuvenated.

Those feelings lasted five days.

Remember the song "Lookin' for Love in All the Wrong Places"? I was looking for joy in all the wrong places and from all the wrong people. The day I finally threw up my hands in defeat turned out to be the first day joy showed up in my classroom.

God is just waiting for us to give up, give in, and give Him the thanks and praise He deserves for each and every day. What is the first step toward this joy He has promised us? Do good unto others. Then God will pour His wisdom, knowledge, and joy into the work of our hands!

Reaping the Harvest

Pleasure seekers rarely find what they are looking for. However, those who do good and seek wisdom will find that and more. Even in the midst of a challenging school year we can find joy. Each day is given one at a time. Before students enter your room each day, spend some time thanking God for each and every one of them. Go down your roll and commit each student to the care of your heavenly Father. It helps refocus your view and your teaching on meeting the needs of those in your care.

Daily Apple

Be a Professional

Frame and hang your diplomas and certificates—from an honor society association, or other recognition or awards—on the wall of your classroom. Doctors and lawyers have their diplomas framed and hanging on their office walls—so should you.

Get business cards. Make them professional looking—*not* cutesy. Put the school telephone number and/or school e-mail address on them for a contact number.

Use school stationery for all correspondence with parents and outside personnel.

12

HERE'S TO YOU, MRS. ROBINSON

An Apple of Gold

Let him who is taught the word share in all good things with him
who teaches. Do not be deceived. God is not mocked; for whatever a
man sows, that he will also reap. For he who sows to his flesh will of
the flesh reap corruption, but he who sows to the Spirit will of the
Spirit reap everlasting life. And let us not grow weary while doing
good, for in due season we shall reap if we do not lose heart.
Therefore, as we have opportunity, let us do good to all, especially to
those who are of the household of faith.

GALATIANS 6:6–10 NKJV

Sowing the Seed

This passage offers a variety of ways and reasons for doing good. First, Paul says that students should take care of the material needs of their teachers, especially those who teach God's Word. If we gain in status or material goods in this world because of those who taught us, we should share our gain with them. Every action has results. If we plant to please God, we'll reap joy and everlasting life. We should be generous with our gifts to one another.

But Paul does acknowledge that it can be difficult, even draining, to do good. This is especially true when we don't feel appreciated or respected. It is easy to lose heart, but if we can persevere in doing good, we will reap a harvest of blessing.

Doing good to others is a practice, something we must actively pursue. We should do good to all but especially to other Christians. It is an important reminder for us to do good to all, not only to our fellow believers.

Who has taught you the Word of God? Instead of waiting for someone else to come along and thank you, look for those whom you can thank. Remember that you will reap what you sow.

Tending the Orchard

Mrs. Robinson was my first-grade teacher. She loved teaching. It was obvious in the way she decorated her room. We could also tell by the enthusiasm she showed while teaching. And we felt it by the way she treated us. She loved us. I knew she loved me.

Having attended public school all of my life, I never experienced a teacher who taught me the Word of God. But there were a few who exemplified it. Mrs. Robinson was the first to do so in my life. It was a devastating blow to discover that she wouldn't be my second-grade teacher the following year. That doesn't make sense to a six-year-old.

I did thank Mrs. Robinson when we parted. I visited her during second grade and told her again how much she meant to me. But then the years passed, and we moved away. It wasn't until years later, when I became a teacher, that I recalled her influence in my life. I looked for her then but couldn't find her.

I wanted my students to feel as safe, as important, and as loved as I did with Mrs. Robinson. When *Apples and Chalkdust: Inspirational Stories and Encouragement for Teachers* (Honor, 1998), my first book, came out, I looked for her again. I wanted to share my success with her. I desperately wanted her to know that without her this book wouldn't have been possible.

Then I discovered that my children's principal knew Mrs. Robinson. He had access to records that I did not. He called me into his office to tell me some astonishing news. Mrs. Robinson, my Mrs. Robinson, had moved to North Carolina years earlier when her husband died.

"May I have her address?" I asked with excitement trembling through my voice.

"I'm sorry, Vicki. She died just two weeks ago," the principal said, his eyes fixed on mine.

I had missed my chance to thank her personally. She never saw *Apples and Chalkdust*. As a teacher, I knew how precious a single word of thanks was. That was the day I stopped waiting for someone to appreciate me. That was the day I decided to look for as many former teachers as possible who had made a positive impact on my life and thank them.

Reaping the Harvest

You can choose today to be the kind of teacher that students will remember fondly as making a difference in their lives. It is for their good that we teach, not our own. Our goal should be to teach in a way that pleases the Father. Only then will He pour His blessings upon us.

Daily Apple

Would you like to find a teacher from your childhood? Visit *www.classmates.com* and see if your teacher is registered with your school or graduating class. Your alumni association or former student council may be registered there and may also be able to help you find a former teacher.

13

A BLAST FROM THE PAST

An Apple of Gold

As cold waters to a thirsty soul, so is good news from a far country.

PROVERBS 25:25 KJV

Sowing the Seed

Receiving good news from a far country is something that kings would wait on. Even in the New Testament, Paul writes to both the Corinthians and Thessalonians, letting them know how wonderful and important it was to receive good news about the churches there. Titus brought news about the church in Corinth, and Timothy brought news about the church in Thessalonica.

Yet Paul wasn't the only recipient of good news. He would send word back to the churches through messengers like Titus and Timothy to encourage them and build them up. At times he would rebuke them through his letters, but often the letters were meant to remind the young churches of the ultimate Good News—that Jesus is the Christ and that He came, died, was buried, and rose again in fulfillment of the Scriptures.

There's something special about hearing or reading a good word from someone far away.

Tending the Orchard

Sometimes it's hard to stay motivated and positive about teaching. There are so many things that discourage us. The rewards are usually few and far between. Sometimes encouragement comes when we least expect it yet need it the most.

I have a manila envelope, torn in some places and bulging as if its contents want to escape. I guess I don't take them out as often as I should. The envelope is full of thank-you notes from the eight years I was a classroom teacher. There are times when I ache for those days. The daily interaction with students always filled my heart with satisfaction and, oftentimes, joy. It's hard to be separated from that life. Yet even now their letters and cards soothe me. I know many of my former students are grown and probably have families of their own, but when I picture them in my mind, they are still twelve or thirteen years old—still sitting in the seats where I left them.

Most of these thank-yous are from parents of students who struggled in school—either academically or behaviorally. They thanked me for my patience, my kind words for their child, or the extra effort I put into bringing him or her up to speed. Years after I left the classroom, I received a letter from a mother of one of my most troubled students. She just wanted me to know that even nine years after her son was in my class, he still referred to me as the "only one who cared" when he was in school. She said it was enough to help him to persevere through technical school later on. How wonderful that news was to me when I was home dealing with two toddler boys.

Realizing how precious good news from a far country was to me, I decided to actively look for and find some of the teachers who had made an impact on my life. I found my third-grade teacher, Mrs. Carol Kurtz, just recently. I vividly remember being in her classroom. Her love for learning was contagious! Here is her response to my e-mail:

> Vicki, what a wonderful surprise to hear from you! And I am even more delighted that you became a teacher and wrote a book! I think it is just terrific. It brought tears to my eyes that you remembered me and that I was an inspiration. You helped fulfill my dreams about having some positive effect on young people. I can only wish you the best and hope that you will have the same kind of satisfaction and joy in teaching that I have had.

Reaping the Harvest

When you receive a good word from a far country, remember that it is God's gift to you. Can you turn around and give that gift to someone else far away? With e-mail anything is possible!

Daily Apple

Find a place that makes custom rubber stamps. Often it will be in a business or office supply store.

Have some of the following stamps made:

- your signature
- Read but not graded
- Graded for content only
- Parent's signature

14

WALK!

An Apple of Gold

*This is what the Lord says: "Stand at the crossroads and look;
ask for the ancient paths, ask where the good way is, and walk in it,
and you will find rest for your souls. But you said, 'We will not
walk in it.'"*

JEREMIAH 6:16

Sowing the Seed

God has told us what we must do in order to find some rest.
Long ago God marked out the path for us to follow. It is the only
true way to peace. Yet we tend to reject God's path and mark out
our own instead. The Israelites defiantly walked their own way.
God warned them again and again to turn back and take the way
already paved for them. They said, "We will not walk in it." They
wanted to take the back roads and even the dirt roads. It's easy to
get lost on those roads! You've heard it said, "It's my way or the
highway!" Why is it that so many of us choose our own way?
God's highway is the only way that will truly lead us to peace and
"rest for our souls."

Tending the Orchard

Teachers don't like being told what to do or how to teach,
especially by someone who is not in the classroom. That even

goes for direction from principals and other administrators. We think we know best and that our way is the better path. I've always wondered what that path leads to. Is it children learning? Or is it our desire to find peace amid the chaos of a school? Whatever it is, I know I've been guilty of defiantly turning my back on the way I knew I should go.

"Just submit to his authority," my husband, Chip, said after one of my many evenings of complaining about my principal.

I felt that my way of handling a recent situation between myself and my principal was better. This man was doing his best to get me to bow down to him, and I wasn't going to do it!

"I know what I'm doing," I said. "I've been down this road before. My way works."

After all, I knew my students better than he did. I knew how to handle difficult students and their difficult parents. I was sure I could handle this difficult principal. Chip wasn't convinced.

"Your way is only going to make you look bad and God look worse. Your principal knows you're a Christian, right?"

Suddenly I felt like I was caught in God's cross hairs. I knew Chip was right. I knew he was only trying to protect me from myself. Yet I pressed on.

"He's playing a game with me," I said. "I can't let him win. It's the only way to find some peace during this school year."

"The only way?" Chip challenged.

I am not a defiant person by nature. In fact, I am normally quite the opposite—compliant to a fault. Peace at all costs—that was my way of handling conflict. But at this time I was weary of the path of least resistance. Yet this battle wasn't giving me any rest either.

In my anger toward this principal, I couldn't even see the path God wanted me to walk. I couldn't find the "ancient way." So I sat down in the middle of the road and cried—defeated and willing to surrender. "What should I do?" I mumbled to my incredibly patient and wise husband.

"Do what he tells you to do. Do it with a humble spirit. Do it as unto the Lord," he said and held me in his arms.

And I did.

God's path isn't always the easiest path. It's usually not the most popular route. In fact, it can be full of obstacles and even detours. But if I maintain the course, I know I will arrive at my destination.

Reaping the Harvest

Are you looking for peace in all the wrong places? Schools are not peaceful places. They are full of uproar and chaos. Where can you find rest for your soul? Not in the teacher's lounge, that's for sure. You are standing at a crossroad. Ask about the ancient path. Then follow it. Before you know it, even during the insanity of lunch duty, you'll be at peace!

Daily Apple

Professional Development

Philosophies of teaching, methods, and challenges have all changed drastically in just the past five years. For teachers who started their careers thirty years ago, it is not the same career today. You must continually change and be knowledgeable about the field to be a professional. In-service seminars, articles, books—all will help keep you current in the field. The key is to be willing to learn.

15

DO NOT GROW WEARY

An Apple of Gold

For even when we were with you, we commanded you this: If anyone will not work, neither shall he eat. For we hear that there are some who walk among you in a disorderly manner, not working at all, but are busybodies. Now those who are such we command and exhort through our Lord Jesus Christ that they work in quietness and eat their own bread. But as for you, brethren, do not grow weary in doing good.

2 THESSALONIANS 3:10–13 NKJV

Sowing the Seed

Do you know anyone whom you would characterize as a busybody? Someone who always seems to have too much time on his or her hands and ends up filling that time with less than helpful activities—like gossip? We could call these people the "under"-employed. In Paul's letter to the Thessalonians, he reminded them of something he had addressed when he was with them. "If anyone will not work, neither shall he eat." It seems that word had reached Paul that there were still people among them whose concentration was not on their work, but on other people's business.

This passage is not only a word to exhort and admonish those busybodies, but it is also meant to be an encouragement to those who already do good; that they may continue, even though those around them do not. What an encouragement that is! We tend to become preoccupied with those among us who aren't doing what they are supposed to do. Suddenly our own focus is off the work we are called to do.

Tending the Orchard

"How does he get away with it?" a particularly bristly teacher said.

"This is the third faculty meeting he's missed," said another with even more venom.

"Do you know that I heard he doesn't even attend his department meetings?" said the first.

"No!"

"Yes. And we are supposed to serve bus duty together this week, and I haven't seen him out there, either," she continued.

This back and forth gossip/complaining went on for another ten minutes. These teachers were sitting right in front of me during our monthly faculty meeting. Needless to say, I couldn't hear what our principal was saying. I had to go up to her after the meeting and get some things clarified. It's a good thing I did, because there were deadlines attached to much of what she said!

These teachers were speaking the truth. The teacher they were complaining about was skipping out on his duty and meetings. I don't know how he got away with it, but it didn't matter. He wasn't my responsibility. My responsibility was to my students.

There is so much to do in so little time as a teacher. It always makes me wonder about those teachers who spend their time comparing notes about who is doing what and pointing their fingers of disapproval. Who has time to do that?

Reaping the Harvest

Are you tired of always doing the right thing when many around you are not? Pray for those who are eating the bread of idleness. But then be encouraged and know that God's blessings fall on those who do well with the work that God has given them to do.

Daily Apple

Getting to Know You

We spend much time getting to know our students. How much time do we spend getting to know ourselves—the person God created us to be? In *Finding Your Leadership Style: A Guide for Educators*,[1] Jeffrey Glanz describes seven virtues all educational leaders should have. Teachers are educational leaders. Meditate on these virtues and get to know yourself and your style a little better, for the sake of your teaching and your students.

1. Courage
2. Impartiality
3. Empathy
4. Judgment
5. Enthusiasm
6. Humility
7. Imagination

I believe God's values for us are found in this list. Strive to develop each in yourself.

16

CONSOLATION PRIZE

An Apple of Gold

Bless those who persecute you; bless and do not curse. Rejoice with those who rejoice, and weep with those who weep. Be of the same mind toward one another. Do not set your mind on high things, but associate with the humble. Do not be wise in your own opinion.

ROMANS 12:14–16 NKJV

Sowing the Seed

Paul offers us some life-changing guidelines about how we should behave toward one another in this passage. Even as fellow believers, we don't always treat each other the way God commands. Things go wrong. People don't get along. Jealousy rears its ugly head. We compare ourselves to others, deciding that we are holier somehow. "Be of the same mind toward one another"—this is not something we have to pretend to be. We are of the same mind. We all have the Holy Spirit dwelling within us. And we are all sinners—the great equalizer.

It always means more to me when I weep that those who weep with me can empathize—they know what it feels like. Yet Paul doesn't say to weep only with those with whom you have a common pain. He says, "Weep with those who weep." It's the Spirit within us that is reaching out to the spirit within that other person. That's all the empathy we need. The same is true for times of rejoicing.

All the things Paul outlined in this passage can be quite difficult for us to do. Notice he didn't say, "Do these things if you feel like it." He knew it was hard; that's why it's a command. You don't usually have to command people to do the easy things. In addition, these are all things that Christ modeled for us while here on Earth. Since we have His Spirit, we are able to follow these commands. It's a matter of submitting our will to His.

Tending the Orchard

I found her crying in the teacher's lounge when I walked in during my planning time. She was on the couch curled up in a ball and sobbing. I froze. I didn't know what to do or what to say.

At that moment all I saw was a woman in pain. Teachers don't usually break down in front of one another, so the fact that Carol was inconsolable there in the lounge was almost frightening to me. I stood silently for another minute at least.

Quietly, I stepped closer to the couch. I knelt next to her and softly asked, "What is it, Carol? Can I help?"

Carol stopped mid-sob but kept her face turned toward the wall.

"What time is it?" was all she could say.

"Five minutes until the bell." I stood and took a step backward.

"Thanks for letting me know." And then she stood and rushed past me into the bathroom.

I decided it would be better if I wasn't in the lounge when she emerged from the bathroom. Obviously this was awkward for both of us. I went out into the hallway and waited. I wanted to make sure she was all right.

When Carol burst out of the lounge, she ran right into me.

Her look of surprise turned into a knowing smile. "Thanks again," she said and quickly disappeared into the sea of students changing classes.

Reaping the Harvest

You don't have to have incredible words of wisdom to weep with those who weep. You don't even have to cry. God's grace can cover our insecurities and inadequacies in this area. Whatever you do, don't turn away from another teacher in pain. You know what the life of a teacher is like.

Daily Apple

Teachers can make an essential difference in the lives of children who learn differently. They can tap the talents of these students by

- understanding the many ways students can learn;
- teaching in a way that addresses learning differences;
- creating a learning climate that supports diversity in learning;
- intervening effectively when students are struggling with learning;
- exploring some ways that teachers can support children with learning differences.

17

IF YOU CAN'T SAY
SOMETHING NICE...

An Apple of Gold

*Don't criticize and speak evil about each other, dear brothers. If you
do, you will be fighting against God's law of loving one another,
declaring it is wrong. But your job is not to decide whether this law
is right or wrong, but to obey it.*

JAMES 4:11 TLB

Sowing the Seed

Some people seem to us more lovable than others. Often it is
difficult for us to love those we may consider unlovable. We find
ourselves gossiping, criticizing, and judging the way they do the
things they do. This passage speaks specifically to Christians
about other Christians. Examine your attitude and actions toward
others. Do you build others up or tear them down? God's law is
to love one another as He has loved us. When you feel yourself
ready to criticize someone, remember God's law of love and say
something good instead. *Saying something beneficial to others will cure you
of finding fault and increase your ability to obey God's law of love.*[1]

Tending the Orchard

I guess the desktop was comfortable, because his head was on
it each and every day. Jay rarely looked up at me, and if he did, it

was with disdain. I was interrupting his beauty sleep! Sleeping in class is a form of rejection to any teacher. It doesn't help us feel good about students when they do this.

I decided I should seek the counsel of his last year's teacher. Maybe together we could figure Jay out.

"He's a slacker. That's all there is to it," she told me in unequivocal terms.

"I don't know him well enough to assume that," I said.

"Well, I do, and believe me, it's a waste of your time trying to reach him."

I was stunned. How could she be so defeatist? There had to be something inside this sleepy seventh grader. I did what my mother always told me to do—I took what this bitter (yet Christian) teacher said with a grain of salt and moved on.

It took persistence, a thick skin (on my part), and praise (a lot of it) to reach Jay. And it took love.

It took more than half of the school year, but Jay finally stayed awake in my class. In fact, he actually did some work on a daily basis. Jay responded to praise, but only private praise. Public praise was humiliating, so I avoided it.

To know God is to love Him. Getting to know Jay didn't help me to love him. I had to love him in spite of knowing him.

Reaping the Harvest

If you know God, you love God. God knows us, and even in our state of being unlovable, He loves us. Because we know God's love, we, too, can love the unlovable—with our words and in our deeds.

Daily Apple

"Beginning Teacher's Tool Box" is a community of educators

offering support to new, student, and substitute teachers through print and online resources. Their books for new teachers have been widely accepted and used by teachers, schools, districts, and universities across the nation. Check them out at *www.inspiringteachers.com/testimonies/index.html.*

18
MAY I HELP YOU?

An Apple of Gold

*Those of us who are strong and able in the faith need to step in and
lend a hand to those who falter, and not just do what is most
convenient for us. Strength is for service, not status. Each one of us
needs to look after the good of the people around us, asking ourselves,
"How can I help?"*

ROMANS 15:1–2 THE MESSAGE

Sowing the Seed

We're not all on the same level of maturity. Some are stronger
in their walk with Christ than others. How do we approach those
who are younger (or less mature)? How do we approach those
who don't know Christ at all? It may not always be convenient to
step in and lend a helping hand. Who does God put in your path
daily, or even weekly? If we are strong in a particular area, we can
use that strength in service to others. Yet we should avoid helping
with our own agenda in mind. Attend to the needs of those
around you. Start by asking, "How can I help you?"

Tending the Orchard

It was open house at my son's fifth-grade classroom. I knew
right away that I liked his teacher. She was organized. She was clear
and concise in her expectations. She loved teaching! And she already

seemed to understand the inner workings of our younger child.

After her talk, we were asked to consider how we could best volunteer this year. She had sign-up sheets at the back of the classroom: drive for field trips, put together Friday folders, and organize class parties. None of those choices appealed to me. I really wanted to work with the kids. Being a former teacher, I missed interaction with students. I didn't sign up for anything.

A couple of weeks went by, and Charles, our fifth grader, started to have some trouble in school. He couldn't stop talking! "I wonder where he got that from?" I said loud enough so my husband could hear. Talking had been the chronic comment on his report cards throughout school. After a conference with the teacher, we had a plan of action.

"Why don't you come in on Fridays and prepare the Friday folders?" his teacher suggested. "I could use another parent to take that on."

It's hard to say *no* when you're asked such a direct question.

Now I prepare the Friday folders *and* watch how my son behaves for about an hour and a half every week. My presence seems to calm him, and he's been able to successfully curb his talking.

I'm glad I didn't get my way about how I volunteer.

Reaping the Harvest

Sometimes we find ourselves waiting around for someone else to meet our needs. Change the focus. Look around instead at whose needs you could meet today.

Daily Apple

Answer Cards

Answer cards are a great way to involve an entire class and

quickly see who's on the right track. For each student, place six or more three-by-five note cards inside a library book pocket. Across the end of each card write one response. I use A, B, C, D, YES, and NO. You may want to add cards with TRUE and FALSE or other responses. The students remove the cards they will need and hold their cards close so no one can see them. Then I state the question and answer options, repeat once, then tell them to think (wait a few seconds); say, "Get your answer ready," and "Now, show me your answer." Everyone's answers must be held up at the same time. You can see in a second who needs help. If many are wrong, say, "Put your cards back and let me give a clue." Then repeat the steps. The kids love this, and they feel successful and involved. *Bonus!* I've done this several times during evaluations, and I never fail to get extra credit for student involvement and motivation.

Submitted by: Claudia, fourth-grade teacher

19

ARE YOU THERE, GOD?

An Apple of Gold

Who shall separate us from the love of Christ? Shall tribulation, or distress, or persecution, or famine, or nakedness, or peril, or sword? As it is written: "For Your sake we are killed all day long; we are accounted as sheep for the slaughter." Yet in all these things we are more than conquerors through Him who loved us. For I am persuaded that neither death nor life, nor angels nor principalities nor powers, nor things present nor things to come, nor height nor depth, nor any other created thing, shall be able to separate us from the love of God which is in Christ Jesus our Lord.

ROMANS 8:35–39 NKJV

Sowing the Seed

Sometimes in the midst of our troubles and trials we may feel alone. Where is God? we ask with urgency. Has he abandoned us? We struggle to understand the truth of the matter—that we are not alone. He cannot and will not ever leave us. His Spirit dwells within us. He is there through it all, through every trial, every persecution, and every attack—physical or spiritual. Paul covers it all in this passage. There is not one thing created (and God created it all) that could separate us from Him. This is one of the most encouraging passages in Scripture. So be of good courage! The Lord, your God, is with you!

Tending the Orchard

It was one of those dark winter mornings. I taught in a portable classroom, and that morning the lights wouldn't come on. I propped open the door with a brick I kept for that purpose and gingerly stepped inside. My eyes didn't adjust quickly enough to see the overturned desk in front of me. I fell to the floor and hugged my shin and knew, even in the dark, that blood seeped through my pantyhose.

When I opened the window shades, which were always drawn at the end of the day to discourage illegal entry after school hours, I shielded my eyes. But it wasn't the welcome light of the dawn that surprised me. It was the destructive and graphic nature of the vandalism my classroom had suffered overnight.

I guess I should not have been surprised at this violation. What did I expect, teaching in an inner-city school in the belly of the projects? I was warned not to arrive early or stay late. I was warned not to drive a car that I cared about to school. I was warned to lock my classroom door even while class was in session. Somehow this invasion felt personal—more than the predictable on-the-job hazards my principal warned us all about.

Where was God when some of my own students broke into our classroom and destroyed everything we had built together that year? Had I stepped out of His will by choosing to teach in such a place? I wept. Not because I had been violated, but because I felt like God was too far away to hold me just then.

Reaping the Harvest

It doesn't have to be a violent act that makes you wonder if God is there with you. It could be when a parent confronts you or your colleagues speak ill of you behind your back. It could be when the lesson you planned fails or your car breaks down on your way to school. But God is there—with you. His Spirit indwells you for this very purpose. Nothing can separate you from Him. It is not possible. Rest in the assurance of that truth.

Daily Apple

The "Creative Teaching" Web site provides educators, teachers, and anyone interested in learning with tips for creative teaching, motivational teaching, and professional development. The site provides insight into teaching methods, styles, and skills for teachers and educators at all student age levels and in all disciplines. Visit them at *www.creativeteachingsite.com.*

20

RICH TEACHER, POOR TEACHER

An Apple of Gold

He who loves money shall never have enough. The foolishness of thinking that wealth brings happiness! The more you have, the more you spend, right up to the limits of your income. So what is the advantage of wealth—except perhaps to watch it as it runs through your fingers!

ECCLESIASTES 5:10–11 TLB

Sowing the Seed

The love of money is the root of all kinds of evil. We see its consequences all around us. The rich man doesn't think he is rich when he looks around and sees someone richer than he. Even one poor person is richer than another. Both rich and poor can love money and spend their time and energy pursuing it. Yet our God is a jealous God, who prefers that we spend our time and energy pursuing Him instead.

We can't serve two masters, God and money. While we agonize over how small the budget is again this year or are crushed by a lack of salary increase, we reveal that our love of money and its provision is where we put our trust. Can we instead trust the God of the universe to sustain us? Can we trust that He will meet our needs according to His riches in heaven? Do we believe that

He will give us exceedingly abundantly more than we ask? People will disappoint us. Putting our trust in people to provide for our needs rarely brings us peace.

Tending the Orchard

Sometimes the money issues that surround education feel like a slap in the face. I certainly felt that way during my first year as a teacher. I knew teachers didn't make a lot of money, but I didn't know you basically took a vow of poverty when you signed your teaching contract.

I was hired just three days before the beginning of the school year, and when it came to a budget and supplies, I inherited whatever the last teacher had ordered. Needless to say, I didn't need much of what she ordered, and there was no money (or so they said) for me to order what I thought my classroom required.

My beginning-teacher salary was meager, and I shared a classroom with another teacher. We both taught learning-disabled students. These students are easily distracted. How well do you think they did sharing a room with another class, separated only by a four-foot-high bookcase? I found out quickly that our principal did not consider my program a valued asset. I did not receive money for textbooks or technology or office supplies. I had money for some art supplies, and that was all.

I spent a lot of my time and energy fuming that year. I don't handle injustice very well, and this was injustice. It took longer than I would like to admit for me to see this as an opportunity to respond God's way.

Reaping the Harvest

Remember, "money isn't everything!" But more important, don't disparage humble beginnings (see Zechariah 4:10). God may be offering you the opportunity to grow first in your faith and second in your budget. And it will be He who receives the credit, not those who lobbied for the increase. Just when you think you can't make it another day without copy paper, a parent donates some. Just when you cut back your supply order, the district releases more money! God will and does use whatever means necessary to show us that He is sovereign and worthy of our trust.

Daily Apple

17 Documents to Keep in Your Professional Records File

1. Your teaching certificate/license(s)
2. Transcripts of degrees and credits, including attendance
3. Letters of hire
4. An individual employee contract if you signed one upon hire
5. Supplemental contracts for extra-duty responsibilities
6. Your local Association's negotiated contract
7. Yearly salary information and payroll notices
8. Records pertinent to your retirement
9. Records of leave accrual and use
10. Evaluation and growth plans
11. Commendations, awards, and honors
12. Teaching schedules
13. Records of incidents involving discipline or referral of students
14. Records of referrals of students with special needs
15. Copies of all correspondence from your employer
16. Proof of Association membership
17. The Association's $1 million liability insurance brochure[1]

21

BECAUSE HE LIVES

An Apple of Gold

The steps of a good man are ordered by the Lord,
And He delights in his way.
Though he fall, he shall not be utterly cast down;
For the Lord upholds him with His hand.

PSALM 37:23–24 NKJV

Sowing the Seed

Who is a "good man"? One who follows God, trusts Him, and tries to do His will. God watches over those who follow Him. He makes firm every step that person takes. There will be times when we stumble, but we will not fall. Or we may fall, but we will not be *utterly cast down*. If we fall into a horrible pit, God will set our feet upon a rock (Psalm 40:2). And when our burdens seem more than we can bear, God is able to lift us up. The key is to follow His ways so that we can count on His hand to uphold us when we fall.

Tending the Orchard

The chicks in our incubator died. One day the chicks were pecking and scratching the bottom of their box and the next they were silent and still. Their softness remained, but the breath of life that we witnessed as it revealed itself from the recesses of the thin pearl-white shells had gone. I've never seen so many grief-stricken faces as I did in my class that morning. These children, the chicks' caregivers, had no answers, only questions.

"Why did they all have to die?"

"What did we do wrong?"

"What do we do now?"

Some cried. Others stomped around the room in angry circles. And still others stood vigil over the incubator as if willing the now-still chicks back to life. They had done everything right. So how could everything have gone so wrong? I had questions of my own.

Their love and compassion for these tiny creatures brightened our classroom each day. Their hopes were dashed and their hearts heavy. My job, on that day, was to somehow communicate that their hearts could be heavy without being completely broken. I wanted them to know that God's love was the only love that sustains life. What I lacked in volume of words I made up for in gentle words and soft touches. They were consoled, and only by the breath of God did life return to my classroom that day.

Reaping the Harvest

Life-sustaining love—that's what God has for us! He can hold us up when we fall. But He can also use us to uphold those in our care so that they may also know that love. There is life for us only because He lives!

Daily Apple

Procrastination: The Number One Enemy

Your work load can be daunting. However, procrastination only results in more work and more pressure. When faced with unpleasant tasks, an overwhelming project, or simply too much to do:

- Set a deadline that is earlier than the absolute deadline.
- Break the project into manageable steps.
- Eliminate unnecessary steps and delegate those that could be someone else's job.
- Be positive; you will finish.
- Recall and use strategies that have worked for you in the past (frequent breaks, early morning starts, etc.).
- Reward yourself for a job well done (a walk, a swim, a long hot bath ...).
- Work with a colleague or mentor. Support each other in managing time. You don't have to do this alone![2]

22

JUST DESSERTS

An Apple of Gold

I the Lord search the heart and examine the mind, to reward a man
according to his conduct, according to what his deeds deserve.

JEREMIAH 17:10

Sowing the Seed

God knows our heart. He's the only one who really does. He actively searches it and examines our thoughts and inner motives. It is so easy to fall into temptation and do or think things without first scrutinizing our own motives. God will examine our motives whether we do or not. Our rewards are based on our deeds. This reminds me of how we wish our students would carefully examine the quality of their work before turning it in to their teachers for grading. We are going to give them a grade based on what they turn in. If they don't have a quality mindset about how they do what they do, they won't think about whether their work is acceptable or not. God desires that we think about why we do what we do. What are our motives? If we haven't considered them, there is a good chance what we present to God may not be pleasing.

Tending the Orchard

Report card time is often a struggle. Many students perform in such a way that assigning their grade is effortless. Others, unfortunately, require more careful consideration. One year in particular some of my students received failing grades. I knew I would get a lot of criticism for these report cards. Parents would probably complain. My principal would call me in and talk to me about the image of my program and how failing grades weren't good for that image. Students, who were used to easily sliding by and still getting a good grade, would be upset.

Teaching middle-school gifted students is a challenge in itself. Pleasing everyone involved with such a program is just not possible. My class was difficult, but these students were able to succeed—they just chose not to. How can I give a passing grade to a student who did absolutely *nothing* in my class? I couldn't. It would have been different if a student had worked hard, only to fail by one point. I would extend grace in that situation. But no such motivation existed in these students. Their hearts were hard.

When students complain about a grade I have given them, I remind them that I am merely a secretary—one who records what they themselves did or did not do. Maybe next time they will examine their own intentions, before a teacher or parent passes judgment on their performance.

Reaping the Harvest

Why do we do what we do? It's a matter of the heart. Before examining the motivation of your students, remember to take a close look at your own motives. The desire to please God will bring His blessing upon you and the work of your hands.

Daily Apple

Explain to parents/caregivers why you need their assistance.

Families need to understand why their involvement is

helpful, as some believe schools expect pupils to complete homework entirely independently. A range of approaches may be required to explain to as many parents/caregivers as possible what you are proposing to do. This might include contact by telephone, personalized letters, specific meetings (consider venues other than the school), using the support of other agencies and community contacts, etc.[1]

23

LIFT IT UP!

An Apple of Gold

*I will bless the Lord at all times; His praise shall continually be in
my mouth. My soul shall make its boast in the Lord; the humble
shall hear of it and be glad. Oh, magnify the Lord with me, and let
us exalt His name together.*

PSALM 34:1–3 NKJV

Sowing the Seed

Our God is worthy of praise all day and every day. Whether
we feel like it or not; whether we are rich or poor; whether we are
great or small—our God is always good. His greatness is what
matters. Our greatness magnifies His. The first few verses of this
psalm remind us of how wonderful and how capable God is. He
promises great blessings to His people, yet our active participation
is required. Before we focus on the promised blessings, let us
gather together and praise His name!

Tending the Orchard

Every prayer group I've ever been a part of laid a list of peti-
tions at the foot of the cross. There's nothing wrong with seeking—Jesus told us that we do not receive because we do not ask.
Teachers know how to pray. We have a lot to pray about. But one
of the most powerful experiences I ever had was not during a

group prayer time but rather when I stumbled into a group praise time.

I was new to this school. I was still trying to figure out how to get copies made by the workroom assistant. One day between classes, I slipped into the teacher workroom to check my mailbox, hoping my copies for the next class were there waiting for me. They weren't. Disappointed, I turned to leave the room, but something caught my attention.

The door to the maintenance closet was slightly ajar. From somewhere inside I heard muffled voices. I snuck a peek just out of curiosity. Crammed inside this six-by-six-foot closet were eight women, some teachers, some staff, huddled together as if they were planning the winning touchdown for a championship game.

"Yes, Jesus!"

"He is worthy!"

"Hallowed be His name!"

Awestruck, I gently pushed the closet door open.

"Excuse me. Is this a private group, or can anyone join?" I asked with a smile.

They enveloped me into their embrace, and we continued to praise the name of Almighty God for five minutes more. Then we returned to our classrooms, still basking in the glow of God's glory. I knew that day no matter what trials came or what blessings were bestowed, my God was in this place!

Reaping the Harvest

When you gather together to ask the Lord's blessing, remember together to lift your praises high. Together we can magnify His name!

Daily Apple

Angela Jackson offers advice on stress management, bringing the calm to the storm of everyday teaching:

"You need balance, so take the holistic view. Arrange your life so that you have time for essential rest and play, as well as work. Take control by managing your time and you will automatically eliminate one of a teacher's worst stress-makers—lack of time."[1]

24

JUST IN TIME

An Apple of Gold

There is a time for everything, and a season for every activity under heaven . . . a time to tear and a time to mend, a time to be silent and a time to speak.

ECCLESIASTES 3:1, 7

Sowing the Seed

The wisdom of King Solomon is unsurpassed by men. His discussion of what is really important in this life is life-changing! Time is short, but I am so glad that there is an appointed time for everything. God's timing is indeed perfect. The key is to synchronize our watches with God. All too often we set our own time and then become frustrated in our attempts to make it all turn out right. Pray for a stillness of heart. Then pray for ears to hear so that we will know what time it is by the sounding of the ultimate timekeeper.

Tending the Orchard

I'm used to being in control. Teachers are the ones in charge—usually. I had a strategy for parent/teacher conferences. My goals were to first focus on the positive; then gain the parent's trust; and then gently reveal any negative aspect with regard to his or her child. Usually by the time our conference was over, I had enlisted the support of the parent and felt certain that together we could eliminate the negative from a student's behavior. But I met my match in Mrs. Johnson.

"I really am grateful for the time you've set aside for this conference," she began. "Josh really enjoys your class." She took a breath, but not long enough for me to jump in.

"You can't imagine how thrilled I am to finally meet you!" Mrs. Johnson was on the edge of her seat. She shifted from side to side as if preparing to enter a moving jump rope.

"I . . ." I almost got a word in—almost.

"You're the first teacher to give our son a chance." And then there was silence.

I looked down at my laundry list of challenges her son presented and then shot up a silent prayer. *Guide my tongue, Father. Choose my words.*

When I looked up again, our eyes met, and in hers I saw reluctant tears.

"I think it's time we make a plan together for how best to help Josh succeed," I began.

Mrs. Johnson relaxed back into her chair and let out a long-held breath.

Reaping the Harvest

You may be just in time to help a student whose time is running out. Be willing to trust God's timing in your life and the lives of your students. You are their teacher at this moment for a very specific purpose.

Daily Apple

Financial Tips for Teachers by Alan Jay Weiss and Larry Strauss[1] is designed especially with educators in mind, offering new insights into financial planning that can make a real difference to today's teachers' lifestyles. The book begins by asking the reader to take stock of his or her current financial situation in the chapter titled "Where Are You Now and Where Do You Want to Be?" It then moves on to strategic solutions for financial success with information on accumulating savings, making extra money during both the summer months and the school year, protecting your investments, and taxes and legal concerns.

25

To Tell the Truth

An Apple of Gold

And you, son of man, do not be afraid of them nor be afraid of their words, though briers and thorns are with you and you dwell among scorpions; do not be afraid of their words or dismayed by their looks, though they are a rebellious house. You shall speak My words to them, whether they hear or whether they refuse, for they are rebellious. But you, son of man, hear what I say to you. Do not be rebellious like that rebellious house; open your mouth and eat what I give you.

Ezekiel 2:6–8 NKJV

Sowing the Seed

The Old Testament prophets were always faced with the task of presenting God's message to ungrateful and abusive people. Ezekiel's challenge was no different. God knew exactly to whom Ezekiel would have to speak His words. He knew that Ezekiel could be discouraged by the rebellious nature of the people. He also knew that Ezekiel could be tempted to walk away from this task because it was too hard. It doesn't matter if those we speak God's words to accept or refuse what they hear. What matters is if we speak them out of obedience to God. People may look at you and shake their heads and say you're wrong or crazy. Just remember, they speak out of rebellion toward God—you speak out of obedience.

Tending the Orchard

There is an unwritten gag rule on teachers. We're not supposed to talk to the press or to *outsiders* about what is wrong in education. Outsiders can include parents. The advent of state testing has made it even more difficult on teachers, whose job has now become that of image maintenance. Putting a positive spin on issues like state testing can often feel like lying.

"Do you agree with the decision to replace the national standardized test with the state test?" This was a direct question from a parent. My mind swirled with competing thoughts. Should I answer truthfully or give the politically correct answer?

"In my opinion, it is too soon to replace the national test," I said, deciding this answer was safe.

"Do you think the state test results accurately reflect what my son learned this year from you?" Oh boy, that was a loaded question. I reviewed all the acceptable answers I was trained to give in such a situation. None of them was truthful.

"I hope so. But I have to be honest; it's hard for me to see a correlation." There—I said it.

"That's what I thought," he continued. "Thank you for being honest."

Now I had to wait and see what the fallout would be from my choice of honesty. At least I hadn't lied. I had to please God first.

Can you speak the truth on a matter without reaping the wrath of your superiors? Probably not. Should the threat of anger or rejection from your supervisors tempt you to say nothing? Sometimes we allow it to. God wants us to speak His truth even if those who hear reject us or, worse, persecute us as a result. He knows we'll be tempted to ignore the situation and walk away. He knows how hard it is when we're surrounded by rebellious people.

Reaping the Harvest

Daily we are challenged to speak the truth—whether it is to students, parents, colleagues, administrators, or the public at large. It may be so much easier to avoid or walk away from the truth, but remember that when you speak, you speak out of obedience to God.

Daily Apple

12 Tips for Communicating With Parents

1. Be certain that anything you distribute to parents in writing is *accurately and professionally done.*
2. *Keep your own record* of everything you put on paper to parents or school personnel. The easiest thing is to keep a copy.
3. For notes, permission slips, reports, requests, and explanations of school activities, *use a form of reproduction that is easy to read* (watch out for worn-out originals and bad copy equipment!).
4. *Avoid grammar or spelling errors.*
5. *Write clearly and concisely* so parents will understand your message. Be accurate on times, dates, and locations.
6. *Avoid education jargon.*
7. *Type your message neatly* or write it clearly in longhand.
8. Send your communication home *far enough in advance* so that parents can act if you expect a response.
9. *Ask a colleague to read your communication* before it goes home to see if it can be improved.
10. *Give a copy to your administrator.*
11. *Set up a system* for getting responses back on items like field trip permission slips.
12. Since much of your direct communication with a parent

or administrator is oral (by phone or in person) with no written record of what was said, *keep a log*. A log is useful for recording . . .

- Feedback to your advice to parents
- Parents' suggestions for helping their children
- Discipline problems and your responses
- Safety hazards and your responses
- Requests for funds for instructional materials
- Requests for curriculum adjustments
- Incidents of vandalism or violence
- Difficulties with administrators and your responses
- Observations and evaluations and your responses
- Symptoms of student drug or alcohol abuse and your responses
- Indications of child abuse or neglect and your responses[1]

26

GOLDILOCKS

An Apple of Gold

*Be patient and you will finally win, for a soft tongue can break
hard bones.*

PROVERBS 25:15 TLB

Sowing the Seed

Proverbs has much to say about the words we choose and how
we use them. Often our natural tendency when we are faced with
those who are hardhearted or hardheaded is to respond to their
words with harsh words. Their hardness is offensive to us. If we
are in a position of authority, their hard words are full of dis-
respect and defiance. Our first reaction might be to crush this
defiance with hard words of our own. Proverbs suggests that a
different approach is called for. First we need to be patient. We
can choose to be slow to anger and give ourselves time to consider
our words before we speak them. Then we can offer soft words to
the hardhearted. This combination of action and words can
change how others respond to you.

Tending the Orchard

Her name was China. She was quite tall for an eighth-grade
girl, but she slumped over so much you forgot her Amazon-like
stature. China's bangs were always too long, and I finally realized

that was intentional. She wanted to be able to look at me through her blond strands without my noticing. I rarely saw her eyes from beneath that mane.

China made a decision early on that she wasn't going to like me. Her only verbal responses to me were in the form of grunts and groans. I barely knew this girl, and she hated me! It wasn't easy to walk into that classroom day after day. I don't handle rejection well, and this student wouldn't even give me a chance.

I held back my words from China. I refused to stoop to her level and speak out of anger or bitterness. I just ignored her, thinking that no interaction was safer. But inside it felt wrong. I became a teacher to make a change for the better in the lives of children. How could I turn away from her?

One day I noticed a beautifully beaded purse on China's desk. I'm a sucker for fine craftwork, so I had to ask: "This is beautiful, China. Where did you get it?"

Silence. Head down; but I knew she was looking at me from behind those bangs.

"She made it," Andrea piped up. Andrea's gift was getting in the middle of everyone else's business.

The next day there was a different beaded beauty on China's desk. She was waiting for me to notice it.

"Did you make this one, as well, China?" Her head bobbed up and down in affirmation. "Well, it's just gorgeous."

On and off throughout the school year new beaded change purses appeared on China's desk as if on display. And on the last day of school I found one such marvel on my own desk. China didn't make an appearance that day, but I knew somewhere she was watching from behind her golden locks to see if I was pleased or not. Indeed, I was quite pleased!

Reaping the Harvest

Softness doesn't mean you're not in charge. Our own personalities could all do with a little more softness in some areas. Oftentimes we are harder on people than we ought to be. Be patient. Think. And then finally speak with carefully chosen words in a softer tone.

Daily Apple

The Power of Self-Reflection

Although the first years of teaching seem to consume you, you do need to stop to reflect on how you are doing. Make short notes about how policies work, how units went, and think about how you treat your students. After all, we are there for the students, and there is more than content to teaching. However, this is difficult to see the first years.

- *Take compliments seriously and criticism lightly.* I feel like I make more mistakes than I do good. But I can't let this get me down. Mistakes are how we learn. Take the compliments you get and put them in a "warm fuzzy" file to pull out on a rainy day.

- *Share, share, and share!* You must have someone to confide in. A spouse or significant other is fine, but it really ought to be someone in the teaching field—a mentor teacher, or even another new or student teacher. Many times just talking about frustrations and joys gives you insight about the situation that you hadn't seen before.

- *Share materials.* Most teachers take it as a compliment that you want to copy their units. It is much easier having something to work from, something to build on, that you can change to fit your teaching style.

- *Write out your philosophy* and have it handy. On days when you wonder why you went into the profession of education, pull it out and remember your reasons for becoming a teacher.

- *Have ways of encouraging yourself.* Maybe it is a favorite poem, story, or audio/videotape. Mine is an audiotape of Guy Doud from a broadcast of Dr. Dobson's *Focus on the Family* radio show. Guy Doud was Teacher of the Year, 1986–1987. He entertains, encourages, and reminds me that I am in the right profession.

- *Take time for non-education reflection.* You need to remain sane for your sake and for your students' sake. Many times it will be difficult to do this, but I found that when I was stressed the most, I wasn't giving myself time to be "off-duty." Enjoy music, quiet time in prayer, and/or moments just to be thankful for what you have.[1]

27

Actions Speak Louder

An Apple of Gold

*Let love and faithfulness never leave you; bind them around your
neck, write them on the tablet of your heart. Then you will win
favor and a good name in the sight of God and man.*

Proverbs 3:3–4

Sowing the Seed

It's not enough just to know what God expects of us. We have
to make it a part of our own character and act upon it. Actions
always speak louder than words, and actions affect others more
deeply. Love and faithfulness are important character qualities. A
loving person not only feels love, he or she also acts in a loving
way toward others. If we are loving and faithful in the eyes of
people, we will please both them and God. A double blessing!

Tending the Orchard

It had been four years since I'd left teaching. Only a few of
the same teachers were still at my school. I went back for a long-
overdue visit, knowing I'd find just a few familiar faces.

Have you ever noticed that schools have a distinctive smell?
Smells evoke powerful memories, and when I walked into my old
school, memories swirled together in my head. I closed my eyes
for just a moment and took it all in—the sounds of students

walking through the hallway and the fragrance of lunch from the cafeteria brought it all back. I felt as if I'd never left.

My last year at that school was one of the best. That first-grade class was especially delightful. The students were all so motivated and couldn't wait to find out what we were going to learn next. They were fifth graders now. I wondered how they were doing.

I didn't have to wait long to find out.

I entered the cafeteria and stood near the door. I smiled to myself, remembering how hard it was to get kids to keep it down to at least a low roar during lunch.

"Mrs. Caruana!" someone shouted from across the room.

Before I knew it, at least a dozen students surrounded me. They were all talking at once. They were my first graders, all grown up!

"Are you coming back to teach here?"

"We missed you!"

"Did you miss us?"

"You were the best teacher I ever had."

Their accolades overwhelmed me. I succumbed to multiple bear hugs and let my joyful tears fall. Four years later my kindness was returned to me—and in a big way!

Reaping the Harvest

If we can live what we believe, not only will we win souls to Christ, we may even experience praise for a job well done from those who don't even know Him—yet.

Daily Apple

Teaching Recipes

As a way of keeping track of all the great ideas I see and read about, I have a recipe box with dividers labeled with different aspects of teaching: bulletin boards, management, organization, Web sites, etc. Whenever I have or find a good idea, I write it on an index card and file it in the appropriate place. I am accumulating quite a few great ideas.

Submitted by: Tara Bigner, Cincinnati, Ohio

28

TEACHER APPRECIATION

An Apple of Gold

Whatever is good and perfect comes to us from God, the Creator of all light, and he shines forever without change or shadow.

JAMES 1:17 TLB

Sowing the Seed

God is frequently pictured as light in the Bible. Conversely, evil is pictured as darkness. Since we cannot create light, anything that is good comes from God. Sometimes we mistakenly believe that we are the masters of our universe. We are not. When we produce good things or receive good gifts, they are creations of God alone. Our accomplishments and achievements all belong to Him!

Tending the Orchard

I've long considered the PTA as the fundraising arm of education. That's all its members seemed to do. They sponsored magazine sales at the beginning of the year, gift and gift-wrapping paper sales during the holidays, and popcorn sales in the spring.

Each year teachers were asked to turn in "wish lists" to the PTA. It always felt to me like making a Christmas list as a child. I knew there was only a slim chance I would actually get something on the list. Making a list somehow lets you think you have some control over the situation, when in actuality you have none. My parents often gave me things that were not on my list. But once in a while they came up with gifts I wouldn't have thought of and ultimately enjoyed.

During February, when our supplies were running low and our morale even lower, the PTA sponsored a mid-year teacher appreciation brunch during one of our in-service days. The food and service were quite a treat. The tables were beautifully decorated, and fine linens and silverware adorned each one. There was a gift bag at each place setting with our name on it outlined in gold calligraphy. I must admit I was genuinely impressed.

After we enjoyed a sumptuous meal, the PTA president explained what they did with the wish lists we gave them.

"Our intention was to choose one or two things from your lists and have them here for you today," she began. "But it was too difficult for us to decide."

We were instructed to open our gift bags. Inside were packets of flavored hot cocoa, some note cards, and a check for $200!

"We decided it was more important that you choose for yourselves how the money we raised should be spent. After all, it's your classroom, and these are your needs."

Now, that's what I call teacher appreciation.

Reaping the Harvest

Even if the PTA president hands you a check, this good and perfect gift comes from God! Sometimes we receive good things when we least expect them or least deserve them. Can you give something good to your students today? Something they wouldn't expect and probably don't deserve?

Daily Apple

Ten things you should never do in a parent-teacher conference . . . and ten strategies for success. Veteran teachers share their dos and don'ts.

1. *Don't* summon parents into the classroom and direct them to sit in front of your desk. *Do* always greet parents warmly at the door.
2. *Don't* begin by focusing on the student's problem. *Do* start the meeting by showing that you care and know something positive about their child.
3. *Don't* dress too casually for the occasion. Some people think casual attire will make the parent feel more comfortable, but experts say that can backfire. You are a professional, and professional attire communicates that message. *Do* dress in a way that reflects the meeting's importance and your respect for the parent(s) and their child.
4. *Don't* wing it. *Do* rehearse what you want to say.
5. *Don't* rely on verbal descriptions of the student's work and progress. *Do* use materials from the student's work folder.
6. *Don't* point a finger at parents or place blame. *Do* use positive, nonverbal behavior.
7. *Don't* dominate a meeting so that parents can't ask questions or make suggestions. *Do* engage parents in planning the best ways to help their child. Seek their suggestions first.
8. *Don't* send them home empty-handed. *Do* give parents something to take home with them.
9. *Don't* use educational jargon or acronyms. *Do* use clear and descriptive terms.

10. *Don't* end the meeting on a negative note by recounting a student's problems. *Do* end positively, with a proactive message of hope.[1]

29

WORRYWART

An Apple of Gold

So do not worry, saying, "What shall we eat?" or "What shall we drink?" or "What shall we wear?" For the pagans run after all these things, and your heavenly Father knows that you need them. But seek first his kingdom and his righteousness, and all these things will be given to you as well.

MATTHEW 6:31–34

Sowing the Seed

We worry about the wrong things. We worry so much about them that our attention to them competes with our attention to God. God knows what we need. He created us. He knows we need food and drink, shelter and clothing. However, if we spend all of our time and energy chasing after the things God knows we need, we will leave God out of our lives. God challenges us to turn to Him first for help when we need it. He wants us to fill our thoughts with His desires. He wants us to pattern our character after His own. He wants us to serve and obey Him in everything. Do these things and He will take care of the rest! That's a promise.

Tending the Orchard

I tried to recall who it was who told me that getting my master's degree would be worth it in the end. I was nearing the end and all I wanted to do was to hunt that person down and put his or her feet to the fire! The stress I experienced over those three years while working full time and taking two classes per semester brought back my stomach ulcers with a vengeance.

I couldn't remember when I last prepared a nutritious meal for my family. When was the last time I read for pleasure? I was sleep deprived and never had time for exercise. Sure, I was learning a lot. In fact, what I was studying was quite fascinating. But I worried about my family. I worried that I wasn't there for them. Then there was the money I was spending to take these courses— no one was going to reimburse me for these expenses.

I couldn't remember the last time I spent quality time with anyone I loved. When was the last time I connected with God? I don't think I had opened His Word once over the past twelve months.

I was attending to the urgent over the important.

Didn't the important deserve equal time—at the very least?

Yet the *urgent* screams for attention; the *important* patiently waits its turn.

God patiently waited. My husband waited. Even my students waited. How long would their patience last?

I couldn't walk away from my studies. But maybe I could walk away from the worry that plagued me.

Reaping the Harvest

Worrywarts don't experience God's peace. He knows what we need. Are you willing to let go of the worry and turn your attention to God and the work going on in His kingdom? Remember the old saying: *Let go and let God.* It has more value than you might think.

Daily Apple

Don't Let It Get to You—Ways to De-Stress Your Teaching

Studies show that as many as 50 percent of teachers leave the profession by the fifth year of teaching. Surely job stress must play a part in this. For those of us who stick it out (even if only to the end of this year), there are things we can do to make our lives a little easier.

1. Have a positive attitude.
2. Do not try to accomplish too many tasks in one day.
3. Relax through stretching and exercise.
4. Get plenty of sleep.
5. Leave your teaching at school as often as possible.
6. Get yourself a hobby.
7. Find things to laugh at.
8. Give yourself positive messages.
9. Finally, remember that teachers are important and valuable to our society. Find comfort in the awesome role you are playing in many people's lives.

30
PREPARE

An Apple of Gold

Fear not, for I have redeemed you; I have summoned you by name;
you are mine. When you pass through the waters, I will be with you;
and when you pass through the rivers, they will not sweep over you.
When you walk through the fire, you will not be burned; the flames
will not set you ablaze.

ISAIAH 43:1–2

Sowing the Seed

Isaiah 43 speaks of God's special love for Israel. He redeemed them and called them by name to be those who belong to Him. God protected Israel in times of trouble. Yet this passage speaks to us, as well. We are special to God, and He also calls us by name and claims us as His own. We are His and bear His name (43:7). It's interesting to note that it says "when" you pass through the waters and "when" you walk through the fire. Times of difficulty will come. We have two choices when they do: We can either drown in them or grow stronger through them. If we try to go through them in our own strength, we are more likely to drown. If we invite the Lord to go with us, He will protect us.

Tending the Orchard

The last time I went through emergency training at a school

we learned the basics of first aid and CPR. Five years later, when I returned to the classroom after having our first child, I was shocked at what was now included in emergency training.

We had the session on basic first aid and CPR, and I wondered why I had to go through it again. Then we had a session on reporting suicide threats and child abuse. Then we had a session about disarming a student in possession of a knife or firearm. Finally, we had a session on what to do in the case of a school shooting with multiple fatalities!

Not only did I experience incredible information overload, I became numb trying to attach relevance to these life-threatening scenarios. Schools are no strangers to violent behavior. I remember getting punched by a student and having a chair thrown at me from across the room. But the level of this training was on a plane of reality I just couldn't accept.

I remembered the incidents of school shootings that swept across the country over the past few years. I wept at the heroics displayed by students willing to stand for God only to be shot down by an enraged peer. Trouble comes, whether we're prepared for it or not. Trouble comes—and I had to ask, "Are you there, God?"

My comfort didn't come in knowing how to wrap a tourniquet or perform CPR or lead my students to safety in the midst of a firestorm. My comfort came only in knowing that I belonged to God. He claims me as His own. He will not leave or forsake me. He will walk with me through the storms that will come. I have to remind myself that He is with me whether He saves me from physical harm or not. Just as Shadrach, Meshach, and Abednego proclaimed before entering the fiery furnace, "If we are thrown into the blazing furnace, the God we serve is able to save us from it, and he will rescue us from your hand, O king. But even if he does not, we want you to know, O king, that we will not serve your gods or worship the image of gold you have set up" (Daniel 3:17–18).

Reaping the Harvest

Train for the eventuality of trouble and trust in God, who is more than able to save you. No matter what comes, you are His and bear His name.

Daily Apple

"The only way education is going to change is if the classroom teacher makes it happen."

—William Glasser, M.D.[1]

Each teacher has the power to change education for the better from the inside out. It starts deep within his or her own soul and works its way out! Education doesn't need reform; it needs renewal, one heart at a time. Look for ways to build up others in your profession so they, too, can be renewed.

31
GOD IS SNEAKY

An Apple of Gold
Our mouths were filled with laughter,
our tongues with songs of joy.
Then it was said among the nations,
"The Lord has done great things for them."

PSALM 126:2

Sowing the Seed

It's a joyous thing to discover how great our God is. It seems like we need to be reminded again and again of His abilities. We marvel at how He weaves the threads of our lives together into an exquisite tapestry too intricate to be made by human hands. He works in perfect harmony—a little in your life, a little in mine, all at the same time, to bring to obvious climax the fact that He is the Maestro.

And when this happens, no matter how infrequently we notice it, it makes us laugh! God works miracles when we're not looking. He prods, guides, and sometimes places us right where we need to be to bring Him glory. God is full of surprises! It is so much fun to see what He does.

Tending the Orchard

One of the reasons I left teaching was to homeschool our two boys. My last year in the classroom was particularly challenging, because I had a principal who outwardly disapproved of my beliefs and educational philosophy. I was happy to go. I was happy instead to teach my own children, whose principal was my husband!

After two years of homeschooling, I wrote my first book about homeschooling. God gave me that opportunity due in part to my leaving the classroom. What a blessing!

Through the grapevine, I found out that my former principal had stomach cancer and was on leave from his school. I sent him a card and shared my faith with him again. I never heard from him.

Later I heard, again through the grapevine, that he could no longer handle the stress of a school and was accepting an administrative position at the district level. I initially thought nothing of it, since most teachers believe that's where those who've forgotten what it's like to teach go to finish out their years.

To my utter astonishment, the next grapevine installment not only made my mouth drop wide open but also made me point to the sky and say, "Lord, what are you thinking here?" My principal was now the homeschool liaison for our district. I feared what he might do to harass our homeschooling community.

Through circumstances I can only describe as strange and unrelated, I found myself speaking at the district's pre-school-year conference about partnering with homeschoolers. My principal was in the audience. It was unnerving. Then he disappeared, and I didn't see him again until the following year at an even more unusual venue.

He was sitting in a lobby looking like an overwhelmed, yet

excited, conferee at our state's annual homeschool convention. He was poring over his convention materials and trying to decide which workshop to go to first. I hesitated at first but then walked up to him and waited for him to notice me.

He was sincerely happy to see me. He said he came to learn what homeschoolers needed and how he could help them get what they needed. He thanked me for the book I wrote (I had sent him a copy) and said that he would appreciate any advice I could give him. I was speechless.

I don't know the state of his faith in God, but I do know that a seed was planted. It was obvious in his very countenance. God didn't have to show me how He'd been working over the years. I still don't know how all the pieces fit together. All I know is that God surprises us when we think we have all the answers. I'm so grateful He's the one putting the puzzle together and not me!

Reaping the Harvest

God is all-knowing and all-seeing. He sees the beginning from the end and the east from the west. Rest in His power. Laugh at his surprises. They are ultimately for His glory, but they are still for you! He knows how to work in your life. You can trust Him.

Daily Apple

Q. Why is it so hard as a teacher to be treated as a professional?

A. As traditional schools operate now, teachers are not treated as professionals. Everyone—administrators, school boards, state departments, the legislature, and the governors' offices—has a hand in telling teachers what they want done, how to do it, and how it will be measured. There is no job that requires professionals more than teaching, yet there is no job in which the people who do it are treated in ways that make it impossible for them to be professional.[1]

32

HOPE FOR THE LOST

An Apple of Gold

While he was still talking to her, messengers arrived from Jairus's
home with the news that it was too late—his daughter was dead and
there was no point in Jesus' coming now. But Jesus ignored their
comments and said to Jairus, "Don't be afraid. Just trust me."

MARK 5:35–36 TLB

Sowing the Seed

Have you ever faced a crisis and felt totally confused, afraid,
or without hope? Jairus did, and he was devastated that his daughter was dead. Jesus' response to the situation gives us all hope:
"Do not be afraid; only believe." From Jesus' perspective there was
both hope and promise. The next time you feel hopeless and confused, try to look at your problem from Jesus' point of view.
Whatever happens on the outside, you can be assured that He is
the source of all hope and promise for you.

Tending the Orchard

One of my best and brightest students changed right before
my eyes. He became withdrawn, dressed differently, and constantly fell asleep in class. His grades barely hovered above failing.
He gave me no indication that something traumatic had happened
in his life. I feared that it was too late to save him.

I always prayed for my students, and Louis occupied a lot of my prayer time that year. Unfortunately, I never saw a positive change in him for the rest of the school year. He slipped silently off the radar screen and became one of those who seem to fall through the cracks. All year I felt as if I were desperately holding on to him only to have him willingly let go of my hand. I didn't understand it.

Logic tells me that there are simply some kids you can't help, but it never stopped me from trying. I stayed after school and offered tutoring for whoever wanted it. I came in early and let students hang out in my classroom or let students stay in my room during lunchtime. I worked hard to build relationships with my students, but a relationship isn't one-sided. It takes two.

When we lose a student, it's like when a doctor loses a patient. In the beginning it is devastating, but then we become desensitized to it. It's the only way to continue doing our job. When students make the conscious decision to shut down and walk away, there's very little I can do to stop them.

Four years after Louis left my classroom, God allowed me a glimpse into his life once again. He was still struggling, but at least he was still in school! Now sixteen, he could easily drop out. That's what everyone expected him to do. Yet he was still there, and according to his tenth-grade English teacher, he was actually putting forth some effort. It wasn't much, but it was enough to remind me that there is always hope. Our God is the God of second chances. I just prayed that Louis would eventually find Him.

Reaping the Harvest

Some of our students face a life without hope, or at least without hope that is seen. We fear for their present and their future. Jesus said not to be afraid—only believe! Our prayers do not fall on deaf ears. Pray to the God of second chances that He will reveal himself to your students and offer them the hope that is everlasting.

Daily Apple

Making Changes

When it's time to make changes to your program, keep in mind that gaining parental support is key to the success of your newly implemented changes. Ask parents to let you know how their children like the new system. Also ask parents to let you know if they notice improvement in their children's work habits after the change. Your goal is to eliminate adversarial relationships with students and keep parents well-informed as to what is going on inside your classroom.

33

THOSE WHO CAN, TEACH

An Apple of Gold

*Who then is Paul, and who is Apollos, but ministers through whom
you believed, as the Lord gave to each one? I planted, Apollos
watered, but God gave the increase. So then neither he who plants is
anything, nor he who waters, but God who gives the increase. Now
he who plants and he who waters are one, and each one will receive
his own reward according to his own labor.*

I CORINTHIANS 3:5–8 NKJV

Sowing the Seed

Some of us plant the seeds of belief when it comes to missionary work. Others come along after us and water those seeds by helping new Christians grow in their faith. Neither is more important than the other, especially when you consider that it is God who gives the increase. It is His vineyard in which we both work. God's work involves different people with different gifts and talents. We are all a part of the same team playing our positions to the best of our abilities. In order to be useful members of this team, we need to set aside our own desire for glory and seek God's glory instead. Our reward will be certain in heaven if we first seek God's approval for how well we perform in our assigned roles.

Tending the Orchard

How discouraging it was to meet a student in the eighth grade who was struggling to the point of defeat. Mike was such a student. Not only was Mike not performing at grade level (actually three grades below), he didn't seem to care anymore if he succeeded or not. At least that is the attitude he presented to the world. Mike made it clear that he expected me to write him off, as well. It was apparent that's what many of his previous teachers had done. It's hard to teach those who seem to us unreachable. We usually prefer to spend effort and time on students who care about improving. Mike's very indifference challenged me to care.

On my most discouraging days with Mike, I reminded myself that God himself chose this child to be put in my care for this school year. There were definitely days when I thought He'd made a mistake. Mike did not respond to my positive reinforcement, the extra time I took with him daily to teach and re-teach a concept, or when I offered him tasks that utilized his unique artistic talents. These were all things that could often reach someone like Mike. But Mike wouldn't budge.

There were days when I had no patience for Mike's defiance. I believed he had decided he wasn't going to learn. He had made a choice. I couldn't change his mind. Those were the days when I was tempted to walk away from him and wash my hands of the whole ordeal. But the Holy Spirit protested within me. He reminded me of God's infinite patience. Yet I was only human, and my patience was finite. Still, I chose to persevere and did not give up on Mike.

The end of the year came and went, and I wondered how Mike would fare the next year. Would anyone care? Would *he* finally care? Was there a teacher out there, handpicked just for him, who would finally break through? I didn't know. I couldn't know. I prayed for his next teacher, that her words would be wise and Mike would have ears to hear. And for a moment, just a moment, I was envious of the teacher who would finally reach Mike. He or she would have the pleasure of seeing him succeed. But God called me to plant seeds in this particular case. He didn't call me to water. That was for another. He didn't call me to reap the harvest—that was for God alone.

Reaping the Harvest

Our successes with students don't always show up this side of heaven. Teach in a way that pleases God, and allow Him the privilege of providing the increase.

Daily Apple

Do you really believe that every child can learn? In order for that to happen you must do four things:

1. Know your students.
2. Know your subject.
3. Know yourself.
4. Remember that students learn differently.

Keep these goals at the forefront, and you will reach your students and be there to enjoy their successes!

34

THE LADY WHO LIVED IN THE TOWER

An Apple of Gold

A man finds joy in giving an apt reply—
and how good is a timely word!

PROVERBS 15:23

Sowing the Seed

This proverb is part of a chapter that teaches us about the difference between a fool and a wise man. This particular verse is indicative of a wise person. It first acknowledges how wonderful it is to say just the right thing at just the right time. The speaker himself finds joy in his speaking. The listener knows what he hears is good. He receives great benefit from hearing the right word at the right time. But how do we know what the right word is and when the time is right? The context of this verse can help.

Proverbs 15:1–2 sets the stage: "A soft answer turns away wrath, but a harsh word stirs up anger. The tongue of the wise uses knowledge rightly, but the mouth of fools pours forth foolishness" (NKJV). The wise are such because they seek wisdom. In gaining wisdom, we then know how to "use knowledge rightly." Seek wisdom first!

Proverbs 15:22 gives us some of the *how to.* "Without counsel, plans go awry" (NKJV). We need the help of others who are like-minded to broaden our perspective and wealth of experience so that we in turn can offer wise counsel to others.

Tending the Orchard

Sometimes as teachers we isolate ourselves to the point that our perspective can become narrow and hard. We don't always see the truth around us. We even see ourselves and our teaching through a distorted looking glass—sometimes better than we are and sometimes not as good as we are. I became quite discouraged one semester in my new position as a gifted-education teacher at our school.

The students were not happy with me as their new teacher. The curriculum was completely new to me. The other gifted-education teachers weren't forthcoming with information, and I felt as though I were trapped in a tower, alone and abandoned. Was I doing a good job? How would I know? Even parents were questioning the decision to place me in this position. It didn't seem to matter that I had my master's degree in gifted education. My being there was a change they weren't flexible enough to accept.

I needed a knight in shining armor to rescue me—or at least come visit me in my lonely tower.

Just before Christmas break, a note appeared in my mailbox. It read, "I peeked into your room today. You're doing a great job!" It was from my principal. Little did he know that he was my knight in shining armor. And I discovered that I didn't really need him to rescue me or even hang out with me in my tower. All I needed was for him to acknowledge that I was there and he thought I was handling tower life well.

Reaping the Harvest

Our heavenly Father wants to be our knight in shining armor. He has given us countless notes of encouragement in His Word. For some of us, they are unopened notes and are even marked "Return to Sender." But they are there nonetheless. Read them for yourself and for others, so that someday you may offer just the right word of encouragement at just the right time.

Daily Apple

The Power of Routine

Children thrive on routine. They feel secure knowing what they can expect. There will be times when you will want to change their routine, and that can create stress and disorientation. I always knew that when I changed students' seats or the total physical arrangement of the room, it would take a while before everyone settled in again.

How we transition students from one academic activity to another is also important. Build in a pattern or routine when transitioning. For example, put a warm-up activity on the board every day, and while the students are settling in to do it, use that time to take attendance or get your materials together. Then use that same activity to introduce your first lesson of the day. Routine helps us to use our time wisely.

35

GIFT-GIVING

An Apple of Gold

Each one should use whatever gift he has received to serve others,
faithfully administering God's grace in its various forms. If anyone
speaks, he should do it as one speaking the very words of God. If
anyone serves, he should do it with the strength God provides, so that
in all things God may be praised through Jesus Christ. To him be the
glory and the power for ever and ever. Amen.

I PETER 4:10–11

Sowing the Seed

We have all been given special gifts and talents. Some of us don't believe that we possess any special gift, but we do. For those of us who are aware of the gifts and talents we possess, we have a responsibility to use them to serve others and not simply for our own enjoyment. When we serve or work using our God-given gifts and talents, we will experience joy in our work. That, in and of itself, is a blessing from God. It is what He desires for us.

If what we do includes speaking in order to educate or encourage, we should keep in mind that those words represent the living God. If what we do is in service to others, we can rest in the strength that God provides to do it. Serving others can become particularly tiresome without many tangible rewards. God's strength is what sustains us as we serve.

Our good works, especially while using the gifts and talents

God has given us, are meant to bring glory to God. As we interact with others, they will see Jesus in us and, we hope, praise God for the help they receive from us. "Let your light shine before men, that they may see your good deeds and praise your Father in heaven" (Matthew 5:16).

Tending the Orchard

Periodically there are students who require every ounce of our effort, and we are still not sure if they will make it. Maybe they're on the wrong path. Maybe they're just not as capable as we would like them to be before they leave us. I worry that my gift of encouragement isn't enough to steady them on the right path. I worry that my talent for teaching isn't good enough. Every once in a while God gives me the blessing of a glimpse into the lives of the students I worried so much about.

I saw one of my former students working in the grocery store. She recognized me right away. At first I was disappointed at the job she seemed to settle on. But then her words revealed an unexpected truth.

"I wouldn't be here if it weren't for you!" she said with a giddiness I didn't understand. I wondered if this was such a good thing.

"Without you I'd be in prison, or worse." Her smile softened my worried look, and I relaxed.

We hugged over the produce she'd been arranging, and when I looked at her again I saw a grown woman who was happy with herself and her choices. I couldn't ask for a better reward.

I've seen many of my students over the years either in jobs I didn't expect or lifestyles I didn't imagine for them. In those moments I realized, through God's grace, that what I gave them during their school years did not go to waste. God redeemed it all!

Reaping the Harvest

When you wonder or worry about whether or not what you give to your students is wasted, remember that it's God's grace that abounds. In our weakness, He is strong. And in our steadfastness, He is glorified. Be faithful with the gifts and talents He has given you, and He will redeem the time and the effort as you use them to serve others.

Daily Apple

Many Arrows in Your Quiver

We all know there is not one right way to teach every student. Effective teachers develop and utilize a variety of approaches that have proven successful for them and their students. So much enters into student learning: their varying abilities, backgrounds, interests, and learning styles all play a part.

Effective teachers are always on the hunt for the solution to the problem: "Why isn't Johnny learning in my class?" They are conscientious about their own learning and also that of their students.

36

TRUTH OR CONSEQUENCES

An Apple of Gold

A truthful witness gives honest testimony, but a false witness tells lies. Reckless words pierce like a sword, but the tongue of the wise brings healing.

PROVERBS 12:17–18

Sowing the Seed

The choice between being wise and being a fool is outlined succinctly in the book of Proverbs. Every word, every action can be classified as wise or foolish. As those who seek after wisdom, we can monitor our own words and behavior based on the guidelines presented in Scripture.

Our words reveal what is in our hearts. It is not always easy, or popular, to speak the truth. Often the truth is met either with rejection or hostility. No one likes rejection, but what is the alternative? To be rejected by others is to be accepted by God. Our goal is to please God above people. Sometimes we are blessed with pleasing people as well, but not always.

The truth brings life—lies bring death. Consider your words carefully before you speak. Ask the Holy Spirit to guide your tongue as you choose your words and to soften the hearts of your listeners.

Tending the Orchard

Teachers make life-changing decisions every day. When a child's grade is borderline, we must decide whether to give her the higher or the lower grade. When we are not able to meet the educational needs of a child, we decide whether or not to pursue additional services for him. When a child's behavior disrupts our classroom continually, we decide how and when to take drastic intervention. The political climate of education dictates that we make decisions that sometimes improve the image of the school over the learning of the child. There—I've said it! These are the hardest decisions.

Jason didn't qualify for the learning disabilities program. I was sure of it. In fact, I was sure even before I tested him. Jason's classroom teacher had no energy to find a way to meet his needs. Jason just needed a little more time and some one-on-one teaching to help him be successful. But his teacher either was not interested or not equipped to make the necessary adjustments to her teaching. Her solution was to refer him for learning disabilities testing and services.

As predicted, Jason did not qualify for services. The results indicated that he was a below-average student working to his potential. There wasn't anything the learning disabilities program could provide better than the classroom teacher could. The staffing committee on which I served had a different opinion. They wanted him in the program whether he qualified or not!

It wasn't the first time I had been confronted with this situation. It was the same old battle—truth versus less than the truth.

I refused to sign off on the placement of Jason into the program. I offered instead to tutor him on my own time. He wasn't my student or my responsibility, and my offer was turned down. The committee assigned another teacher to the case and placed him in the program anyway. I wished they could see that this decision cost Jason more than it cost them. But they didn't have eyes to see it.

Reaping the Harvest

Struggling with an ethical dilemma? Ask God to give you the strength to do what is right, regardless of what is popular or politically correct. He will help you stand up for the truth!

Daily Apple

Continuous Improvement

What is quality?

Competence + Improvement = Quality

Quality is doing more than is expected. We can expect and nurture quality on two fronts:

We can expect quality from our students.

We can expect quality from ourselves.

Strive to set your students up for success, and you will gain it. Students rise to our expectations. If you expect more, you will get more. In order for quality work to be produced, students must first be competent. That is your number-one priority. Then and only then can you lead them to improve and reach quality.

Pursue your own competence as a teacher. You may be teaching a subject new to you. Gain competence first. Then objectively look at your performance and find ways to improve. If you care about your performance as a teacher, students recognize this caring and will feel supported and encouraged in their own quest for quality.

They are two sides to the same coin.

37

JUDGE AND JURY

An Apple of Gold

*Then I commanded your judges at that time, saying, "Hear the cases
between your brethren, and judge righteously between a man and his
brother or the stranger who is with him. You shall not show
partiality in judgment; you shall hear the small as well as the great;
you shall not be afraid in any man's presence, for the judgment
is God's. The case that is too hard for you, bring to me,
and I will hear it."*

DEUTERONOMY 1:16–17 NKJV

Sowing the Seed

Good leadership is hard to find these days. Qualifications for
leadership have changed since the days of Moses, but what he
outlined in this passage and others in Deuteronomy lends food
for thought for leaders today.

Whether or not justice is served is subject to great debate in
our society. We know injustice when we experience it! Partiality is
the rule of the day. The meek and the mighty are *not* treated the
same. If we are in leadership positions, we would do well to follow
Moses' advice. God is the ultimate judge, but here on earth we
are granted the opportunity to hear cases and render a decision.
It is not an easy thing to do.

Sometimes we go to the opposite extreme and judge more
harshly those who do not deserve it. Maybe they were privileged

in the past. Maybe they have never gotten in trouble before. Judges sometimes make examples of those cases because they do not fear confrontation or retribution. It is not justice.

God is the only completely righteous judge. Allow Him to rule in your heart so that you will rule justly here on earth.

Tending the Orchard

I learned early on not to get in the middle of a fight between students. When I taught in a middle school with an enrollment in excess of fourteen hundred students, I observed numerous student *encounters* on a daily basis. Every day I struggled with whether or not to turn a blind eye to the situations. Fear for your own safety can be a pretty powerful motivator.

It was always easy to pick out the troublemakers. But I began to notice my own prejudices surface during hall or lunch duty. Some kids looked like they wanted trouble. Previous experience taught me that was where trouble usually began.

I only caught the end of the fight, but there were two boys entangled on the floor, encircled by an enthusiastic crowd of onlookers. I shouted from a safe distance for them to stop. I wasn't surprised when no one listened. But I couldn't walk away. I stood there, paralyzed by both fear and a convincing sense of inadequacy.

The roar of the vulturous crowd lessened, and I timidly approached the scene. The eighth-grade hoodlums were both trying to catch their breath. It provided me with a hole to step into.

After the finger-pointing over who started it, I directed them both to the office. The bell rang and the crowd dispersed—all except for one other boy, who followed us to the office.

"He didn't start it," he began.

I didn't believe him. Can you guess why?

"Don't you believe me?" he pushed.

It was hard to—he looked like trouble, too.

At that moment I looked into his eyes—really looked into them. He was pleading with me for a chance. Why was I being so stubborn? When had I become so hardened? This realization scared me. I was in no position to judge this situation fairly.

I dropped them all off at the principal's office and told the secretary that I hadn't witnessed who started it and was in no position to fairly judge the situation. She looked at me with indifference and herded them all into the principal's inner office.

Reaping the Harvest

It's so hard to be a righteous judge—sometimes too hard. Keep your eye on God, the only truly righteous judge, for direction. Follow His lead. Watch closely for your own inadequacies or prejudices before someone else points them out. Your credibility depends upon it.

Daily Apple

Teachers can read minds; did you know that? We know that when a student looks down when we ask a question that he or she doesn't know the answer. The internal world of students is full of emotions, opinions, and notions about life and school. We know they think things like:

"I hate math."

"English is hard."

"I can't draw."

"This class is boring."

We can build rapport with our students by "reaching inside" their heads when we know students will react to what we are teaching. You could preface a lesson they may not easily understand or be thrilled with by saying:

"You might be thinking, 'This isn't very important.' I used to think that, too."

"You might be wondering, 'When will I ever use this?' I've thought of a way."

"You might be asking yourself, 'Isn't there an easier way to do this?' If there is, I'll find it for you."

"You might be thinking, 'This is a waste of my time.' Well, it's only a waste of time if it takes longer than it needs to."[1]

38
THE WAGGING TONGUE

An Apple of Gold

A gossip betrays a confidence, but a trustworthy man keeps a secret.

PROVERBS 11:13

Sowing the Seed

Wagging tongues are rarely life-giving; they tend to steal the joy from others instead. Proverbs has much to say about the use of the tongue. We are so often tempted to let it loose without supervision. If not kept bridled, it will cause harm—sometimes irreparable harm. The traits of a fool include foolish words. Gossip is a collection of foolish words, to say the least.

Why do we gossip? It's usually because we have too much time on our hands. Those who become idle wander "from house to house ... saying things they ought not to" (1 Timothy 5:13). I often wonder how someone could have so much time when there always seems to be so much to get done.

Instead we must strive to be trustworthy and good stewards of our words and our time. If there is a secret, keep it. A trusted friend is valued above all others.

Tending the Orchard

The teaching profession is full of gossip! Teaching is an overwhelming, under-appreciated job. Who has time to gossip? There never seem to be enough hours in the day to get everything done in the first place, yet some teachers find the time to wander around wagging their tongues.

As you may suspect, this is a sore spot with me. It's hard enough to teach students not to gossip and to keep the confidences of their friends. The least we can do as adults is to be responsible for our own tongue and our own character.

Reaping the Harvest

How can we keep ourselves from gossip? Here are a few practical suggestions to follow: Avoid the teacher's lounge if you can. The longer you remain there, the more you may be tempted to gossip. Make sure your own work is done before you go "visiting." And if someone confides in you, keep that person's confidence.

Daily Apple

Reaching the Hearts of Students

"If only I could get into their hearts!"

You can.

The heart is the gateway to the mind. There are a variety of entry points into the hearts of students.

Be with your students. There is power in your presence. Invest your time in your students, because what they really need is you! Don't use seat work as a way for you to get your other work done. Walk around the room. Stop at a student's desk and ask how they're doing. Let them know you are there if they need you. Always be available. If you look too busy, they won't come to you when they are having trouble.

Connect the cognitive to the kinesthetic. Do more than tell your students to tell you if they are confused. Find out for yourself. Take the time to privately check with students who you know struggle, and touch their hearts with kindness. Put your hand on their shoulder (or whatever touch is appropriate) and let them know you care.

Deposit values and lifelong learning. You are your students' role model when they are in your charge. Show them what you value by the way you conduct yourself. Let them see your own love for learning in your passion and excitement for teaching.

Display these heart characteristics as often and as freely as you can: care, compassion, forgiveness, understanding, patience, kindness, humor, and appreciation.[1]

39

SUPPLY AND DEMAND

An Apple of Gold

You gave abundant showers, O God; you refreshed your weary
inheritance.

PSALM 68:9

Sowing the Seed

We are a part of the inheritance of God. Sometimes we grow
weary doing the work God has for us. We know that we belong
to Him, but we feel the weight of this world all the same. After
all, it's here that we live—for the time being.

God is not unaware of our struggles. In fact, at just the right
time He showers us with blessings. We receive what we really need
right when we need it. God gives in abundance.

David lifted up the name of the Lord in this psalm of praise.
David knew what it was like to be weary and brokenhearted. He
shows us the great contrast between how worn out he felt and
how refreshed God made him. God is the giver of what is good—
always (James 1:17).

Tending the Orchard

Starting in a new school is a mixed blessing. It's always great
to have a fresh start, and it gives you the opportunity to begin
again with a clean slate. There are always challenges, though, that

can derail your intent to do a great job.

As the new teacher in a school, you take the room you're given. You hope that there are enough desks, chairs, and supplies. Once I entered my new classroom for the first time and there was no teacher's desk, nor any promise of one in the near future!

If the previous teacher left in a hurry, the storage cabinet(s) may be in disarray or even empty. A supply order has been placed for the new school year, but since you didn't make out that order, you may not get what you need. That was the case for me.

I looked at the pile of supplies that was delivered to my room and sighed. *What I need isn't here,* I thought. I then separated the supplies into two piles—things I might use and things I didn't need. Guess which pile was bigger?

I put the supplies I didn't need on a media cart and wheeled it through the hallway. I stopped in each classroom and asked if anyone was willing to trade supplies. I knew that it was too late to order what I needed. No one took me up on my offer, and I returned to my classroom with my cart still full and my spirits plummeting.

I began to carefully stock the shelves of one of my storage cabinets with all these things I didn't need. When I opened the second one I was dismayed to discover it full of leftover supplies from the previous teacher. It would take hours for me to sort through the rubble before I could put any more of my supplies away.

Tucked behind a box of old ditto paper, I found a treasure. There were four boxes of unopened dry erase markers, two boxes of newsprint, two boxes of computer disks, and three boxes of white poster board! It was a gift. It was a tremendous blessing. It was more than I could have asked for or expected. God certainly gives in abundance, and He gave it at a time when I was most discouraged.

Reaping the Harvest

Since every good and perfect gift comes from God, don't forget to praise Him. Praise Him aloud to all those around you. Let them know that your God fulfills your needs.

Daily Apple

Super Teacher!

Becoming a teacher of excellence is a long process—a journey. No matter what your own education has been or how marvelously you maintain discipline in the classroom, super teachers aren't born, they're made.

It is encouraging to realize that you don't have to be perfect just yet. Learning to teach is a time-consuming, labor-intensive process, not unlike our journey to becoming Christlike.

The difference comes when you look at yourself as a career teacher and not a year-by-year teacher. Remaining a learner yourself opens you up to the opportunity to someday become a super teacher!

40

THE GREAT ESCAPE

An Apple of Gold

I said, "Oh, that I had the wings of a dove!
I would fly away and be at rest—
I would flee far away
and stay in the desert;
I would hurry to my place of shelter,
far from the tempest and storm."

PSALM 55:6–8

Sowing the Seed

Do you ever feel so overwhelmed with the problems of life that you want to run away? Maybe you feel there is no way out. Maybe you feel your enemies are about to triumph over you. David knew that feeling all too well. He also knew there was only one true place of shelter: under the shelter of God's wings.

God is our refuge and our strength. He implores us to enter into His rest. We can find safety and rest right where we are, even while in the midst of trial or trouble. The storm may swirl around us, but we can rest knowing our God shelters us—just as a trusting child can fall asleep in the midst of a torrential rainstorm while in the arms of his mother or father.

Tending the Orchard

My Bible sat on my desk at school for weeks without my even once opening it. My desire for this school year was to begin each day before the students arrived with a quiet time—fifteen minutes, that's all. I guess that was expecting too much!

Somehow, every day something urgent would steal my attention, and before I knew it, the first bell had rung and the students were filing into the room. I would tell myself just what Scarlett O'Hara said: "Tomorrow is another day." But with each passing tomorrow, school became more and more hectic. The stress level rose to heights uncharted for me in the previous years. On top of it all, I was pregnant with our first child and I was tired, very tired. Meanwhile, my Bible had a layer of dust on it that said, "Read me and rest."

Then the unthinkable happened. Midway through my pregnancy, the baby stopped growing and I lost her over the Christmas break. As the day approached to go back to school, my head was swimming with anxious thoughts and fears that tempted me to quit. I just wanted to disappear. I wanted it all to stop. I wanted—no, needed—a rest. But there is no rest for the weary or the brokenhearted. I returned to work.

My Bible was still on my desk, right where I had left it, when I entered my classroom. I sat and stared at it in the quiet of the early morning. I arrived early in order to avoid the discomfort of colleagues who didn't know how to comfort me. I opened God's Word for the first time in months and then frantically pored over the psalms. Little by little my frenzied pace slowed and I began to take real breaths. God met me at my place of need and sheltered me beneath His wings. I didn't even notice my students walk in and quietly surround my desk. When I looked up into their eyes, eyes that wondered if I was all right, I felt safe and ready to greet the day.

Reaping the Harvest

When you walk through the hallways of your school and feel like what you really want to do is run away as fast as your feet will carry you, take that as a sign that you are in desperate need of a safe haven from the storm. You don't have to leave school to find that shelter. God is right there, waiting for you to run under the shelter of His wings!

Daily Apple

Lunch Bunch

Even middle-schoolers like the opportunity to get close to their teachers. I know our lunch time is precious to us, especially since it is so short and rarely uninterrupted. Perhaps you could sponsor a "teacher lunch bunch" once a month. It could be based on cafeteria behavior. It could be a reward for those with perfect attendance that month. It may reward those who have turned in their homework every day (regardless of the grade mark on it). Invite those students to join your monthly lunch bunch. Make being with the teacher a special thing!

41

GOOD NEWS, BAD NEWS

An Apple of Gold

He who corrects a scoffer gets shame for himself, and he who rebukes a wicked man only harms himself. Do not correct a scoffer, lest he hate you; Rebuke a wise man, and he will love you. Give instruction to a wise man, and he will be still wiser; Teach a just man, and he will increase in learning. The fear of the Lord is the beginning of wisdom, and the knowledge of the Holy One is understanding.

PROVERBS 9:7–10 NKJV

Sowing the Seed

How do you respond to criticism? Your response indicates whether you are wise or foolish. If you immediately throw back an insult at someone or put down a person when rebuked, you may find yourself in the company of fools. Try to listen to what is being said instead. There's a good chance there is credibility to the criticism. Learn from your critics. The wise accept instruction and become even wiser. What is the first step to gaining wisdom? To know God. Strive to get to know Him better and better. That is the path to wisdom. Then you will know how to answer others.

Tending the Orchard

I stared at my annual evaluation in disbelief. As a first-year teacher I was already sensitive to criticism, but this evaluation from my principal was a devastating blow to my ego.

Does not redirect student misbehavior. I ignored it. Wasn't that what I was taught to do first?

Did not perform an ending review. He was only there for fifteen minutes! I wasn't done with my lesson yet.

Offers only general praise. How could I be specific when there was nothing to be specific about?

Did not have materials prepared. The office didn't make me enough copies of my handouts. Whose fault is that?

He obviously didn't know what he was talking about. I don't even think he was paying attention to me when he was observing me. In fact, this was the first time all year my principal stepped foot into my classroom. Before he showed up, I was doing just fine.

Do I sound a little defensive? I was.

It took a couple more days for me to process my evaluation. First I went through denial, then sadness over my performance, then acceptance that there might be something to it, to finally a conscious decision to improve. The stages of grief served me well.

By the time I met with the principal to conference about the evaluation, I was in a much better emotional state. I had ears to hear. I am glad that I didn't open my mouth the day I received the evaluation. I would have been seen as a fool.

Reaping the Harvest

Bad news is never fun to hear. But sometimes truth is embedded in it. Be open to criticism. Accept instruction. A good teacher is always learning.

Daily Apple

You've Got Mail!

We all like to get mail (well, as long as it's not junk mail). Children are no different. Every grading period, send out cards to some of your students so that by the end of the school year every child will have received a personal note from you. Make it a note of encouragement, or tell students how glad you are that you are their teacher. Coming from a teacher, this gesture can make a tremendous difference—not only with the student, but with the parents, as well.

I still have a postcard my first-grade teacher sent me in 1969. I treasure it to this day. I moved away and she remembered me.

42

THE SCHOOL OF HARD KNOCKS

An Apple of Gold

No discipline seems pleasant at the time, but painful. Later on,
however, it produces a harvest of righteousness and peace for those
who have been trained by it.

HEBREWS 12:11

Sowing the Seed

The book of Proverbs says that the man who hates correction is stupid (12:1). Here in Hebrews, the author readily admits that discipline, or chastisement, is not pleasant. In fact, it's painful! The important thing is how we respond to discipline, keeping in mind that it is a loving Father who administers it. We can accept it with resignation. We can accept it but believe we really don't deserve it. We can be angry and bitter toward God. Or we can accept it gratefully—the appropriate response we owe Him. We teeter between all of the responses at one time or another. If we can accept discipline gratefully, we have a better chance of being at peace in the future and producing good works. Anger and bitterness produce neither of these.

Tending the Orchard

I discipline my own children not because I want to ruin their fun but because what they are doing leads to danger or disgrace.

I do it because I love them and want them to be safe and to do good. I know this is true, so why is it so hard for me to remember that my heavenly Father wants the same for me?

One year I moved into a position of authority when I left the classroom for a time to become the assistant to the supervisor in my department. That led me to work in the administration building. I believed that this was where the power lay. This was where all the decisions were made. I was excited about the prospect of being in a place where I could really make some changes for the teachers in the classrooms.

However, it didn't take long for me to make my first big mistake as an administrator.

A camcorder was missing from one of our programs in a nearby elementary school. I was told to investigate the possible theft and find out who was responsible for the camcorder. My first point of contact was the assistant principal at the school. Much to my delight it was someone I had taught with years earlier and felt comfortable with. After a few minutes of pleasant reminiscing, I asked Dan whose responsibility it was to monitor the use of technology equipment in his school.

Before he could answer, I said, "Obviously, whoever it is didn't do a good job. If he or she had kept a careful eye on the equipment it wouldn't go missing like this. Maybe someone else should be assigned to this task in the future. The supervisor's office isn't at all happy at how this theft could happen in the first place." I think I said that all in one breath. Then I sat back, satisfied that my position of authority on this case was well understood.

"I was in charge," Dan started. "And I don't appreciate your insinuations."

Two minutes later I stood outside his office as the door slammed in my face. It didn't dawn on me right away that I might be in trouble.

Back in my office I found out.

My supervisor proceeded to give me a long speech about "how things work around here." I was reprimanded. I don't handle discipline well. It devastates me. I held back the tears as his words pummeled me into the ground. When he left, my mind considered various scenarios.

1. I could quit right then and there and leave him high and dry!
2. I could quietly continue doing my job and keep my mouth closed.
3. I could confront my supervisor that the way he handled "teaching" me was uncalled for.
4. I could swallow my pride and walk forward and do the best job I could do.

I could feel the Spirit leading. Number four was the right answer. Not the easiest, but the right one.

Reaping the Harvest

The school of hard knocks certainly hurts! After getting over the initial sting of correction, decide to learn from the situation and move forward in submission to God and humility toward human authority.

Daily Apple

"Voluntarily change assignments periodically. Try a new subject, grade level, or school. People, like plants, grow better if they are repotted from time to time!"[1]

43

LEAD, AND THEY WILL FOLLOW

An Apple of Gold

He who keeps instruction is in the way of life,
but he who refuses correction goes astray.

PROVERBS 10:17 NKJV

Sowing the Seed

A love for learning doesn't come only as a result of successes—failure is just as powerful a teacher. When we fail, we need to be open to instruction, and sometimes even reproof, in order to become successful. This proverb encourages us to accept instruction as the way of life.

Just as a rider nudges his horse in the right direction, God directs our path. Sometimes we need to wear blinders so we won't be distracted. Sometimes we need a bit in our mouth to remind us which way to turn. Other times we need the crack of the whip or the sting of spurs to get us going on the right path. Even though we are not horses, and God is not a rider, we know that an obedient horse is a testimony to its master. If we love God's instruction, we are a testimony to Him.

Tending the Orchard

Teachers are leaders, but we don't only lead students, we lead other teachers. How we handle a particular situation is carefully observed. If we choose the wrong path, there's a good chance another teacher will feel justified in following that same path.

When a new principal comes to a school, it creates conflicting emotions and points of view. Teachers who are more loyal to the previous principal than to the school may leave to follow that principal. If teachers don't agree with the way the new principal handles things, they may try to undermine his or her authority.

"Can you believe it? She wants us to turn our lesson plans in to her every week."

"Who does she think she is?"

"Well, I'm not doing it."

"It's not that big a deal; I don't really have a problem with it," I said.

"Well, you're the only one!"

I sat there trying to decide what to say next. It felt as though they were drawing a line in the sand, and my foot was hovering over it.

"You do whatever you want, but I'm not comfortable defying the principal's authority." There, I'd said it. And I walked away before they could respond.

It's so easy to get caught up in the gripe sessions in the teacher's lounge. They never lead to peace.

Reaping the Harvest

The authorities God puts in our lives are there to instruct and at times to correct us. Our principal, our supervisor, our department head, and even parents have a purpose in our lives to help perfect us before God. Remember that it is His instruction we are receiving; receive it willingly and don't lead others astray.

Daily Apple

Letter of Introduction

Here is an idea that is not for every situation, but it could be very interesting. Encourage parents to write you a letter of introduction for their child. Here's an example of a letter you could write them:

Dear Parents,

It will be my pleasure to be Mary's teacher this school year. I look forward to having her in my class. Would you please consider writing me a letter of introduction for Mary?

Thank you,

Mary's teacher[1]

The better you know your students, the better able you will be to teach them!

44

Fair Warning

An Apple of Gold

*I have told you all this so that you will have peace of heart and
mind. Here on earth you will have many trials and sorrows; but
cheer up, for I have overcome the world.*

John 16:33 TLB

Sowing the Seed

Jesus did all He could do to prepare His disciples for the time
when He wouldn't *physically* be with them anymore. In the same
way He tries to prepare us to walk through this life without His
physical presence so that we may be courageous in spite of the
struggles and trials that are certain to come. Sometimes we wonder
if we struggle in vain. Sometimes in the midst of terrible trials
we feel completely abandoned. But Jesus reminds us that He is
always with us and that the ultimate victory has already been won!
There is nothing in this world too big for Him.

Tending the Orchard

The teacher who was previously in my position warned me
there'd be days like this! I taught sixth-grade severely learning-disabled
students in an inner-city school. It was my first teaching job. I
was excited, but everyone around me was full of gloom and doom.

"Don't get here early or stay late."

"Don't bring a car to school that you care about."

"Never visit a student at his home."

"Don't get in the middle of a fight—you're the one who'll get hurt."

"Don't expect parents to show up for anything!"

I decided they had to be kidding. It couldn't be as grim a situation as they painted it. Could it?

At the end of October the school sponsored an open house night. It was my first open house, and I spent a lot of time preparing for it. I lovingly displayed my students' work around the room. Every surface was spick-and-span. I had sign-up lists for parent volunteers on the table. I even had refreshments all baked from scratch.

I was nervous. Would they like me? Would they approve of my program? Would they think I could actually meet their child's learning needs? I was a classic first-year teacher—desperate for love and approval. I opened my classroom door and waited for parents to arrive.

But no one showed up. Not one parent—all evening.

At the end of the night, I carefully put away all that I had just as carefully prepared. My colleagues said not to take it personally, but I did. I felt rejected.

The three years in that school were disappointing. Not because I didn't teach well or because my students didn't learn. I was disappointed that the families in our area didn't seem to care about their children's education. That is something extremely difficult to combat.

Reaping the Harvest

There will be times when you will feel unsupported and find yourself standing alone. Parents will not support you. Students won't respect you. Even other teachers may not extend their friendship to you. Yet you are not alone. You are not overcome. Jesus is right there in the midst of it with you, and He has already overcome the world!

Daily Apple

Do you remember when you received a lower grade than expected? Do you remember not knowing why you got the grade you did or how you could improve the next time? When students fail, tell them where they can turn for help and how they can still reach their goals. Good teachers never leave students wondering.

45

DAILY DILEMMAS

An Apple of Gold

I gain understanding from your precepts;
therefore I hate every wrong path.
Your word is a lamp to my feet
and a light for my path.

PSALM 119:104–105

Sowing the Seed

The journey each of us is on has the same final destination, but each path is unique. It is also uncharted territory. It's not as if we've been this way before and can retrace our steps. Each step is new. How then can we know which way to go? Especially since we are walking through a dark forest on our way.

God's Word makes us wise—it helps us know which way to go. True wisdom comes from allowing what God teaches to guide us. God's Word illuminates the way!

Tending the Orchard

I attended a good college of education at a state university. I was accepted into the honors program and graduated with honors. I had wonderful internship experiences. Yet it didn't matter in the end where I began my teaching career: in a budget-poor inner-city school or a budget-fat suburban school. Almost daily I had decisions to make that none of my experiences prepared me for.

To me, teaching wasn't just a job, it was a responsibility. Every time a student disobeyed or did not complete his or her work, I was faced with a decision about how to handle the situation. Would my choice be life-giving or would it turn the student off? Every time a colleague whined and complained about a decision made by the principal or district and sought my opinion on the matter, I was faced with the choice to support her opinion and gain a friend, or dispute it and gain an enemy.

Daily there were moral and ethical dilemmas. Daily there were choices that would affect the future of students. Daily there were chances to build or destroy relationships. It was hard to know which way to turn. I felt as if I were gingerly walking through a minefield, in the dark, unsure of my footing with every step.

God's wisdom is the only wisdom worth pursuing and following. It is the only wisdom that works for all people in every circumstance. When I turned to a colleague for advice, there was a chance that it would not be in line with God's Word. It would not lead to life. Sometimes another Christian teacher would speak God's wisdom and help light the way. But if I didn't know what God's Word said on a matter, how would I know whether another's advice was good to follow?

Reaping the Harvest

Wisdom is the prerequisite to all decision making. Keep in mind that the wisdom you receive from textbooks, workshops, and even seasoned veterans doesn't compare with God's wisdom. Seek it daily. Proverbs says it best:

> If you accept my words and store up my commands within you, turning your ear to wisdom and applying your heart to understanding, and if you call out for insight and

cry aloud for understanding, and if you look for it as for silver and search for it as for hidden treasure, then you will understand the fear of the Lord and find the knowledge of God.... Then you will understand what is right and just and fair—every good path. (Proverbs 2:1–5, 9)

Daily Apple

I remember my tenth-grade English teacher. He used to give us compositions to write, but he would give us specific subjects. I didn't write on the subjects he gave us. Rather than give me an "F," he said he appreciated my creativity. I remember him because he didn't squelch me.

—Rob Reiner, movie director/actor[1]

Everyone remembers a teacher who made a positive impact on his or her life. Whom do you remember and why?

46

Peer Pressure

An Apple of Gold

Just because something is technically legal doesn't mean that it's spiritually appropriate. If I went around doing whatever I thought I could get by with, I'd be a slave to my whims.

1 Corinthians 6:12 the message

Sowing the Seed

We have freedom in Christ. Freedom from the power of sin and guilt. Freedom to use and enjoy anything that comes from God. And every good thing does come from God. The Bible does not address each and every possible thing that is good or bad for us. We must use our judgment. If drinking alcohol is legal and permissible, drinking it in front of someone who is an alcoholic is not appropriate. If we have the freedom to do something but it could hurt someone else or lead others astray, then we need to choose not to indulge in it.

Some things are "appropriate" in a given job or in a given group of people; that doesn't mean they are spiritually appropriate for us. We can and should be in control of our impulses. Self-control is a fruit of the Spirit.

Tending the Orchard

Peer pressure doesn't disappear from our lives when we become twenty-one. It is not contained in the walls of a high school. It always has been and always will be a part of human life. Sometimes that pressure comes from the most unexpected places.

I had the luxury of choosing my own curriculum when I taught middle-school gifted students. I had standards to meet, but I was given the freedom to choose what I thought would best meet and even exceed those standards. Students gained their reading credit through my class, so an offering of classic literature was an expected part of the course. I love literature and couldn't wait to share that love with my students.

Book banning was a pretty common occurrence during the 1980s. School libraries faced a barrage of criticism from parents and the surrounding community. Every teacher I knew at the time was extremely cautious in choosing reading material for their students. Committees were formed to "discuss" teachers' choices. Little by little teachers' decision-making power diminished. Yet I still had a choice to make.

I wanted to use a curriculum that focused on short-story classics and provided students with a wide array of discussion topics. This curriculum sparked critical thought and lively debate. It was just the thing to engage their curious minds. But some of the stories weren't "politically correct." In one story I wanted to use, the main character dies, and in another a child finds himself living alone on the streets. In still another, a brother and sister stand by and watch their parents being killed by a pride of lions (*The Veldt* by Ray Bradbury). They were incredible stories with great lesson potential.

I circumvented the parents and presented the stories to my students anyway. I was right; the students engaged in lively discussions and wrote incredibly relevant essays in response to their reading. However, following each story that I was a little worried about, parents would call and complain. My principal supported my choices and told the parents so. Even though I knew that the students were gaining valuable insight and expertise dealing with these classic stories, I felt a twinge of guilt.

I acted out of defiance. I admit it. I didn't want parents telling me how to teach. I stubbornly held on to any shred of decision-making power I had left. My victory was hollow. I know now that just because I was justified in making the choice that I did, it didn't mean that I should have. I was a good teacher, but I wonder if those parents could see Christ in me.

Reaping the Harvest

Although God is not our peer, His pressure is the only kind we should be concerned about giving in to. When something is right in the eyes of others, it doesn't necessarily mean it's truly right for them ... or for us.

Daily Apple

How do you stay energized as a teacher? I don't only mean with regard to teaching but with regard to physical energy, as well. Teaching is exhausting work. Some of us never sit down during the entire school day. The mental and emotional energy it takes to maintain student discipline and quality teaching drains our physical reserves. If we don't take care of ourselves, we will be of no use to anyone—including our own families.

To increase your energy, try to incorporate one or more of the following into your day:

- Don't skip breaks!
- Practice stretching exercises.
- Walk during your lunch break, if possible, or before the school day begins.
- Eat a good lunch (bring it from home) that includes protein

to give you an energy boost for the afternoon.
- Limit your caffeine intake to one cup/drink per day.
- Give yourself a mental break. Read your Bible or daily devotional before students arrive or after they leave.

47

THE REASON FOR THE SEASON

An Apple of Gold

*Therefore do not let anyone judge you by what you eat or drink, or
with regard to a religious festival, a New Moon celebration or a
Sabbath day. These are a shadow of the things that were to come; the
reality, however, is found in Christ.*

COLOSSIANS 2:16–17

Sowing the Seed

The opinions of other people tend to affect what we do and
how we do it. But Christ has set us free of the opinions of others.
Even in the early church, people struggled with judging how others worshiped, what they did or didn't eat, or what religious holidays (holy days) they kept. Old Testament laws, holidays, and
feasts were still observed by Christian Jews, even though there was
no reason for it. Paul calls them a "shadow" of the reality of what
was to come—Christ.

How we worship is not as important as whom we worship. If
fellow Christians hold traditions or ceremonies different from our
own, we don't need to criticize them. However, in our attempts
not to offend anyone, many have taken an all-or-nothing stance:
We celebrate everyone's holy days—whatever the beliefs—or none
at all.

Tending the Orchard

I read the memo in disbelief.

No outward display of any particular religious holiday observance in the month of December.

I wondered what would happen if I displayed Christmas decorations in November instead? I couldn't believe that it had come to this. I thought of Miss Robbins and wondered if she would be allowed to include traditional Christmas hymns in this year's *Winter Celebration* (that's what we call it now). Miss Robbins is a Christian, too.

I thought of the students in my class. It certainly was a mix of races and religions. Even when I was growing up, how to celebrate the holidays was an issue. I grew up in a predominantly Jewish neighborhood, but we sang both Christmas and Hanukkah songs at the holiday concert. We decorated the school and each classroom with both a Christmas tree and a menorah. We had matzo to eat and eggnog to drink. It all seemed perfectly normal to me. I knew different kids celebrated differently. It didn't bother me.

I don't know how the grown-ups handled it. Maybe they struggled with judging one another, as well. But here, in my school, I felt that ignoring the holidays was sad. Admittedly, it would be difficult to include everyone's traditions in our school, but I know some schools try. I applaud them.

I decided to test the intent of that memo.

I'm not much of a bulletin board maker. I'm not creative enough to ever make it look like anything special. But kids are unabashedly creative, so I let them take the lead. I gave them two weeks to put something on the bulletin board that represented what the season meant to them. They did it, not me.

The day before winter break the bulletin board was alive with color and decoration. I was amazed that every child found a way to express his or her observance of this holiday season. It spurred questions from child to child. It was impressive to say the least.

One child, Daniel, noticed everything. And he noticed that there was something missing.

"Mrs. Caruana, where's your decoration?"

At their insistence, I cut out something that represented my beliefs and stapled it to the bulletin board. It wasn't the only cross on the board.

Reaping the Harvest

You can teach tolerance without diluting Christianity. Different people, different lands, all have the same Creator—whether they know it or not. Respect the rules of your school regarding holiday observance, but find a way to then respect the observances of the students in your charge.

Daily Apple

Looking for more ways to improve teacher/student relations? Get involved with students outside of school. Attend some of their activities, sports, or concerts. Show up on their turf. If you see your students hanging out in the mall on a Friday night, don't avoid them. Notice them, and even if they don't show it right there and then, they will be glad you did.

48

NO NEWS IS GOOD NEWS

An Apple of Gold

He who has clean hands and a pure heart,
who does not lift up his soul to an idol
or swear by what is false.
He will receive blessing from the Lord
and vindication from God his Savior.

PSALM 24:4–5

Sowing the Seed

God values honesty. Telling the truth isn't always the easy choice. Sometimes when telling the truth could cost us something, make us uncomfortable, or show us in an unfavorable light, dishonesty comes easier. Yet a blessing is promised from the Lord, and vindication, if we live by honesty out of the pure motive to please Him.

Tending the Orchard

The first time I caught a student cheating I was horrified, I was indignant, and I was swift to administer punishment. I didn't humiliate the student by making him an example to the class. I handled it quickly and quietly. Only the two of us knew what had transpired.

He knew that there were specific steps to take before life

could go on as usual. First, the test was taken away from him. Then I gave him a different form of the test and had him complete it in the remaining time. Finally, as soon as class was over I walked him to the assistant principal's office to formally report his cheating.

After school, content that I had handled the situation properly and convinced this student would think twice before cheating in my class again, the assistant principal called me into his office.

"I talked to your student, but I'm not going to issue a formal discipline referral on him," he said.

I didn't respond right away. He was serious. Nothing was going to be done with this student; his parents weren't even going to be informed.

"Well, I can handle it myself, then," I offered. "I'll call his parents and deal with it."

"I'd prefer if you didn't do that," he said. Even though it sounded like a suggestion, I knew it was an expectation.

"I can't just ignore what he did," I protested.

"Yes, you can. There have been too many discipline referrals so far this semester," he said with insistence.

He didn't have to explain. I knew what he meant. He meant that it didn't look good for the school to have so many referrals. That log was public record.

What this assistant principal essentially did was take away any power I had to punish cheating in my classroom. But it was out of my hands. The ball was in his court, and he decided he wasn't going to play anymore.

It was a rude awakening. It shook my confidence in my school's administration. It made my job much harder, as I had to find ways on my own to maintain discipline in my class. But I decided that if I was asked directly about the incident, I would tell the truth—referral or no referral.

Reaping the Harvest

The truth about lies is that they only lead to more lies. The sin of omission is still a sin. Just because we don't say it out loud doesn't mean it isn't so. Even if it makes you unpopular or uncomfortable, always speak the truth in love.

Daily Apple

Have you ever considered making home visits to your students? Good teachers don't hide in the school. If your students live in a rough neighborhood, take along a friend or ask a counselor or social worker to join you. If you can't visit every family, at least visit the homes of all newcomers and those students who are seriously falling behind.[1]

49

THE SEASONED TEACHER

An Apple of Gold

Walk in wisdom toward those who are outside, redeeming the time.
Let your speech always be with grace, seasoned with salt, that you
may know how you ought to answer each one.

COLOSSIANS 4:5–6 NKJV

Sowing the Seed

Non-Christians are "those who are outside." Daily we have the opportunity to share the Good News of salvation with them. There are ways to communicate God's love and the truth of His salvation without being offensive. You may be in a place that does not allow the clear presentation of the Gospel. How, then, can you share the Good News?

How we say something is extremely important. The message can easily be lost on the listener if our tone of voice is offensive or combative. If we want others to hear what we have to say, it must be "seasoned with salt"—tasty enough that the listener wants to hear more.

Tending the Orchard

Following the "letter of the law" doesn't always secure cooperation or success. Effective communication skills are key to getting your message across—as well as having a receptive listener.

Sometimes as teachers we are missing one or both of those components no matter how well prepared we are or how justified we may feel.

Candy's grades were slipping little by little as the school year went on. She was a pleasant, bright fifth grader who was now unusually reluctant and depressed. I was worried about her. I tried to encourage Candy to keep trying. I tried to find out if there was something going on at home to explain the change in her behavior and attitude—no response.

Candy was in my gifted program and her reevaluation was coming up. This meant that she would be tested to see if she still belonged in the program. This was especially necessary for students who were struggling or who had decided they didn't want to be in the program anymore.

Candy's mom was a fellow gifted teacher in our district, and I admit to having been more than a little intimidated by that fact. I didn't know her mother very well, and what I did know about her made me nervous. She was well-known and respected in our profession, but upon our first meeting she seemed too aggressive for my comfort level. I usually avoid contact with such people if possible. In this case, I made a terrible mistake when I avoided Candy's mom.

I followed protocol and issued the paper work required to have Candy reevaluated. I did my job just as outlined in the gifted-education handbook. Within days I found myself in a meeting with Candy's mom and the principal of our school. It wasn't pleasant.

My principal didn't back my decision to reevaluate Candy. It was obvious that she and Candy's mom were friends. I was alone in my convictions. Needless to say, the reevaluation was cancelled, and Candy did not improve in my class. There was now a huge rift between me and Candy's mom.

I know I messed up. I know that my avoidance of Candy's mom didn't help the situation. I allowed my fear of confrontation to discredit my professional expertise and any relationship I might have had with a parent of one of my students. I lost a chance to share God's love with them all.

A teacher is continually learning—I learned a big lesson that year.

Reaping the Harvest

Our relationships with others may not begin with the presentation of the Gospel, but they can lead to it. Take the time to nurture your relationships with those who are "outside," so that when you do have the opportunity to tell them the Good News, they will be ready to receive it.

Daily Apple

Rules

Setting classroom rules is the very first thing you do each year. Some students will likely question those rules and try to make you dilute them. Avoid any hint of questioning, hesitancy, timidity, uncertainty, pleading, or negotiating. If students think there's a chance you can be swayed, they will take it! Take your rules seriously and your students will, too.

50

SHEEP AMONG WOLVES

An Apple of Gold

I am sending you out like sheep among wolves. Therefore be as shrewd as snakes and as innocent as doves.

Be on your guard against men; they will hand you over to the local councils and flog you in their synagogues. On my account you will be brought before governors and kings as witnesses to them and to the Gentiles. But when they arrest you, do not worry about what to say or how to say it. At that time you will be given what to say, for it will not be you speaking, but the Spirit of your Father speaking through you.

MATTHEW 10:16–20

Sowing the Seed

Jesus prepared the disciples for persecution in this passage. He compared the opposition of the Pharisees to raging wolves! As sheep, our only hope in the face of such opposition is to seek the protection of the Shepherd. We will face such hostility when we choose to follow Jesus. How should we then respond to this hostility? We don't need to worry about what we are to say or how we should say it. The Holy Spirit will give us what we need in that moment. He will speak through us. We must be wise in our dealings with those who oppose us, but harmless as doves.

Keep in mind that it is God who sends us in among the wolves. But He doesn't send us in alone. His Spirit lives within us. So we are never alone, and we are always prepared to speak His Word.

Tending the Orchard

If you're a Christian teacher in a public school, you may believe you are there as a result of deliberate choosing or by default. In God's view, there are no accidents. You are there because that's where He wants you to be. There were times when I thought I was the only Christian in my school, what I would call the "token" Christian. I was the only one who spoke up in opposition to a decision I felt wasn't honorable or one of integrity. I felt very alone. But I wasn't the only Christian in my school.

Gradually God revealed other believers to me over the course of the school year. As our friendships blossomed and we felt safe with one another, I asked a question that had bothered me for a long time. "Why don't you speak up?" They were afraid—afraid of the persecution that might result from their Christian candor.

We can be visible and verbal without being arrogant or antagonistic. It is a delicate balance. God's plan for us in this situation is twofold. Our responsibility is to be wise as serpents but harmless as doves. His responsibility is to give us the words to speak to those who persecute us, when we need them.

Reaping the Harvest

A lamb, even one who finds itself alone in the wilderness, is still under the watchful eye of the shepherd. Rest in the knowledge that your Shepherd, when the time comes, will speak through you to the wolves. It is His Spirit within you they persecute. But you don't have to wander in that wilderness alone. Reach out to another teacher who believes just as you do and hold fast to the promises of God. For He promised that even when you feel persecuted, you can be assured that He will not forsake you (2 Corinthians 4:9).

Daily Apple

Teacher isolation is a commonly cited problem in our schools. School culture is both unique and complex. If you are a beginning teacher or a teacher having difficulty, reach out. Don't wait for someone to assign a mentor to you. Find one for yourself. Look for a teacher whom you respect and whose style and personality matches your own. When considering a mentor, ask yourself these questions:

1. What is my greatest need as a teacher? With what do I need help?
2. Does this person excel where I am weak?
3. Is this person genuinely enthusiastic about teaching?
4. Is he or she considered an exemplary instructor?
5. Am I willing to openly share my problem with this teacher?
6. Am I willing to listen openly to his or her advice?

If you need help, find someone who is doing what you want to do, and ask him or her how he or she does it!

ENDNOTES

Chapter 2
1. Robert D. Ramsey, *501 Tips for Teachers* (New York: McGraw-Hill Books, 2003), 144.

Chapter 4
1. Adapted from Ronald L. Partin, *Classroom Teacher's Survival Guide* (San Francisco: Jossey-Bass, 1999), 13.

Chapter 5
1. Parker J. Palmer, *The Courage to Teach* (San Francisco: Jossey-Bass, 1998).

Chapter 6
1. Ron Burgess, *Laughing Lessons* (Minneapolis: Free Spirit Publishing, 2000), 13.

Chapter 7
1. Todd Whitaker, *Motivating and Inspiring Teachers* (Princeton, N.J.: Eye on Education, 2000), 47.

Chapter 8
1. Adapted from Myra Felton, *The Busy Teacher's Book* (Lincolnwood, Ill.: Publications International, Ltd., 2000), 16.

Chapter 9
1. Rob Abernathy and Mark Reardon, *Hot Tips for Teachers* (Tucson, Ariz.: Zephyr Press, 2002), 18–19.

Chapter 10
1. Adapted from Cheryl Miller Thurston, *Survival Tips for New Teachers* (Fort Collins, Colo.: Cottonwood Press, 1997), 21.

Chapter 15

1. Jeffrey Glanz, *Finding Your Leadership Style: A Guide for Educators* (Alexandria, Va.: ASCD, 2002).

Chapter 17

1. *Life Application Bible*, New King James Version, (Wheaton, Ill.: Tyndale House Publishers, Inc., 1993), commentary, 2280.

Chapter 20

1. *www.nsea-nv.org/teachersmain.htm*.

Chapter 21

1. *Life Application Bible*, New King James Version, commentary, 952.
2. *www.nsea-nv.org/teachersmain.htm*.

Chapter 22

1. *www.standards.dfes.gov.uk/homework/parentalsupport/tipsforteachers/*.

Chapter 23

1. *www.sparkisland.com/public/articles/stress busting/?view=teacher*

Chapter 24

1. Alan Jay Weiss and Larry Strauss, *Financial Tips for Teachers* (Performance Learning Systems, 1995).

Chapter 25

1. *www.vtnea.org/ti–3.htm*.

Chapter 26

1. *www.iloveteaching.com/steacher/success/new.htm*.

Chapter 28

1. Adapted from *www.nysut.org/newyorkteacher/backissues/1998–1999/981007parentconference.html*.

Chapter 30

I. William Glasser, *The Quality Schoolteacher* (New York: HarperPerennial, 1998), 10.

Chapter 31

I. Glasser, *The Quality Schoolteacher*, 10.

Chapter 37

I. Rob Abernathy and Mark Reardon, *Hot Tips for Teachers* (Tucson, Az.: Zephyr Press, 2002), 50–51.

Chapter 38

I. Abernathy and Reardon, *Hot Tips for Teachers*, 81.

Chapter 42

I. Robert D. Ramsey, *501 Tips for Teachers* (New York: McGraw-Hill Books, 2003), 180.

Chapter 43

I. James D. Sutton, *101 Ways to Make Your Classroom Special* (Pleasanton, Tex.: Friendly Oaks Publications, 1999), 45.

Chapter 45

I. David Shribman, *I Remember My Teacher* (Kansas City: Andrews McMeel Publishing, 2001), 19.

Chapter 48

I. Ramsey, *501 Tips for Teachers*, 127.